First World War
and Army of Occupation
War Diary
France, Belgium and Germany

57 DIVISION
171 Infantry Brigade
King's (Liverpool Regiment)
8th Battalion
1 February 1918 - 31 May 1919

WO95/2983/5

The Naval & Military Press Ltd
www.nmarchive.com
Published in association with The National Archives

Published by

The Naval & Military Press Ltd

Unit 10 Ridgewood Industrial Park,

Uckfield, East Sussex,

TN22 5QE England

Tel: +44 (0) 1825 749494

www.naval-military-press.com

www.nmarchive.com

This diary has been reprinted in facsimile from the original. Any imperfections are inevitably reproduced and the quality may fall short of modern type and cartographic standards.

© Crown Copyright
Images reproduced by permission of The National Archives, London, England, 2015.

Contents

Document type	Place/Title	Date From	Date To
Heading	WO95/2983/5 57 Div 171 Infantry Bde 1/8 Kines Liverpool Regt Feb 1918-May 1919		
Heading	57 Division 171 Bde 1/8 Kings Liverpool Regt 1918 Feb-1919 May From 55 Div 164 Bn		
War Diary	Waterlands Camp B.2.c	01/02/1918	05/02/1918
War Diary	Pont De Neeppe B.23.b	06/02/1918	14/02/1918
War Diary	Pont De Neeppe	15/02/1918	28/02/1918
Operation(al) Order(s)	8th (Irish) Batt "The King's" (L'Pool R) Operation Order No. 1	01/02/1918	01/02/1918
Operation(al) Order(s)	8th (Irish) Battn "The King's" (L'Pool Regt) Operation Order No. 2	05/02/1918	05/02/1918
Operation(al) Order(s)	Operation Order No. 3 8th (Irish) Bn K.L.R.		
Operation(al) Order(s)	8th (Irish) Bn "The King's" (Liverpool Regiment) Operation Order No. 3	07/02/1918	07/02/1918
Operation(al) Order(s)	8th (Irish) Battalion "The King's" (L'Pool R) Operation Order No. 4	10/02/1918	10/02/1918
Miscellaneous	Administrative Instructions With Reference To Operation Order No. 4		
Operation(al) Order(s)	8th (Irish) Battalion "The King's" (Liverpool Regt) Operation Order No. 5	14/08/1918	14/08/1918
War Diary	Bourecq	01/03/1918	16/03/1918
War Diary	Caudescure	11/03/1918	21/03/1918
War Diary	Nouveau Monde	22/03/1918	26/03/1918
War Diary	Heurbaix Sh.36.N.W.H.21	27/03/1918	31/03/1918
Operation(al) Order(s)	8th (Irish) Battalion "The King's" (Liverpool Regt) Operation Order No. 9	20/03/1918	20/03/1918
Miscellaneous	Administrative Instructions With Reference To Operation Orders No.9	20/03/1918	20/03/1918
Operation(al) Order(s)	8th (Irish) Battalion "The King's" (Liverpool Regt) Operation Order No. 10	25/03/1918	25/03/1918
Miscellaneous	Administrative Instructions With Reference To Operation Order No. 10	25/03/1918	25/03/1918
Operation(al) Order(s)	8th (Irish) Battalion "The King's" (L'pool Regt) Operation Order No. 11	28/03/1918	28/03/1918
Miscellaneous	Administrative Instructions With Reference To Operation Order No. 11	28/03/1918	28/03/1918
Heading	57th Division 171st Infantry Bde War Diary 8th Battalion The King's Liverpool Regiment April 1918		
Miscellaneous	Headquarters 57th Division	01/05/1918	01/05/1918
War Diary	Fleurbaix	01/04/1918	01/04/1918
War Diary	Estaires	02/04/1918	02/04/1918
War Diary	Le Souich	04/04/1918	04/04/1918
War Diary	Warlincourt	05/04/1918	11/04/1918
War Diary	Terramesnil	12/04/1918	12/04/1918
War Diary	Pommera	13/04/1918	13/04/1918
War Diary	Authie	14/04/1918	16/04/1918
War Diary	Pas	17/04/1918	30/04/1918
Operation(al) Order(s)	8th (Irish) Batt "The King's" (L'pool Regiment) Operation Order No. 12	01/04/1918	01/04/1918

Miscellaneous	Administrative Instructions With Reference To Operation Orders No.12	01/04/1918	01/04/1918
Operation(al) Order(s)	8th (Irish) Batt "The King's" (Liverpool Regt) Operation Order No. 13	02/04/1918	02/04/1918
Operation(al) Order(s)	8th (Irish) Batt "The King's" (L'Pool Regt) Operation Order No. 14	08/04/1918	08/04/1918
Operation(al) Order(s)	8th (Irish) Batt "The King's" (L'Pool R) Operation Order No. 16	12/04/1918	12/04/1918
Operation(al) Order(s)	8th (Irish) Battalion "The King's" (L'Pool Regt) Operation Order No. 17	14/04/1918	14/04/1918
Miscellaneous	8th (Irish) Battalion "The King's" (L'Pool Regiment) Operation Order No. 17	14/04/1918	14/04/1918
Miscellaneous	General Instructions Issue With Reference To Operation Order No. 17	14/04/1918	14/04/1918
Miscellaneous	General Instructions With Reference To Operation Order No. 18	15/04/1918	15/04/1918
Operation(al) Order(s)	8th (Irish) Battalion "The King's" (L'Pool Regiment) Operation Order No. 18	15/04/1918	15/04/1918
Operation(al) Order(s)	8th (Irish) Battalion "The King's" (L'Pool R) Operation Order No. 19	16/04/1918	16/04/1918
Miscellaneous	To all Recipients of O.O. No. 20	21/04/1918	21/04/1918
Miscellaneous	To All Recipients Of General Instructions With Reference To Operation Orders No.18 And 20	23/04/1918	23/04/1918
Miscellaneous	8th (Irish) Batt. "The King's" (L'pool R). Appendix "A" To O.O.20. Appendix "A" To O.O.20.	23/04/1918	23/04/1918
Miscellaneous	8th (Irish) Batt. "The King's (L'Pool Regt)	23/04/1918	23/04/1918
Operation(al) Order(s)	8th (Irish) Batt "The King's" (L'Pool Regiment) Operation Order No. 20	25/04/1918	25/04/1918
War Diary	Pas 57D 1/40000 C.17.b	01/05/1918	06/05/1918
War Diary	Gommecourt E.29	15/05/1918	15/05/1918
War Diary	Chateau De La Haie 57 DNE.J.6	17/05/1918	17/05/1918
War Diary	Coigneux J.9.a	18/05/1918	21/05/1918
War Diary	Gommecourt	21/05/1918	31/05/1918
Map	Map		
Miscellaneous	War Diary	01/07/1918	01/07/1918
Operation(al) Order(s)	8th (Irish) Battalion "The King's" (L'Pool R) Operation Order No. 23	05/03/1918	05/03/1918
Operation(al) Order(s)	8th (Irish) Batt "The King's" (L'Pool R) Operation Order No. 24	14/05/1918	14/05/1918
Miscellaneous	8th (Inf) Br K.L.R.	17/05/1918	17/05/1918
Operation(al) Order(s)	8th (Irish) Battalion "The King's" (L'Pool R) Operation Order No. 26	20/05/1918	20/05/1918
War Diary	Gommecourt	01/06/1918	07/06/1918
War Diary	Couin	08/06/1918	14/06/1918
War Diary	Gommecourt	21/06/1918	30/06/1918
Operation(al) Order(s)	Operation Order No. 32 8th (Irish) Bn King's L'Pool Regt	06/06/1918	06/06/1918
Miscellaneous	Administrative Instructions With Reference To O.O.32		
Miscellaneous	Administrative Instructions Issued With Operation Order No. 33	10/06/1918	10/06/1918
Operation(al) Order(s)	8th (Irish) Battalion "The King's" (L'Pool Regt) Operation Order No. 33	10/06/1918	10/06/1918
Operation(al) Order(s)	8th (Irish) Battalion "The King's" (L'Pool R) Operation Order No. 34	13/06/1918	13/06/1918

Miscellaneous	8th (Irish) Battalion "The King's" (L'Pool R.)Administrative Instruction Issued With Operation Order No. 34		
Operation(al) Order(s)	8th (Irish) Bn "The King's" (L'Pool Regt) Operation Order No. 35	20/06/1918	20/06/1918
Miscellaneous	Administrative Instructions Issued With Operation Order 36	28/06/1918	28/06/1918
Miscellaneous	Headquarters 57th Division	03/08/1918	03/08/1918
Operation(al) Order(s)	8th (Irish) Bn "The King's" (L'Pool R) Operation Order No. 36	28/06/1918	28/06/1918
War Diary	Chateau De La Haie Rf 57.D.N.E	01/07/1918	02/07/1918
War Diary	Bois de Warnimont	02/07/1918	15/07/1918
War Diary	Henu	16/07/1918	28/07/1918
War Diary	Sus-St-Leger	29/07/1918	29/07/1918
War Diary	Etrun	30/07/1918	30/07/1918
War Diary	Trenches	31/07/1918	31/07/1918
Operation(al) Order(s)	8th (Irish) Battalion "The King's" (L'Pool Regt) Operation Order No. 101	01/07/1918	01/07/1918
Miscellaneous	Administrative Instructions With Reference To Operation Order 38	01/07/1918	01/07/1918
Operation(al) Order(s)	8th (Irish) Battalion "The King's" (L'Pool Regt) Operation Order No. 39	14/07/1918	14/07/1918
Miscellaneous	Administrative Instructions With Reference To Operation Order No. 39	14/07/1918	14/07/1918
Operation(al) Order(s)	8th (Irish) Battn "The King's" (Liverpool Regt) Operation Order No. 40	28/07/1918	28/07/1918
Miscellaneous	Administrative Instructions With Reference To Operation Order 40	28/07/1918	28/07/1918
Operation(al) Order(s)	8th (Irish) Battn "The King's" (Liverpool Regt) Operation Order No. 41	30/07/1918	30/07/1918
Miscellaneous	Administrative Instructions Issued With Operation Order No. 41	30/07/1918	30/07/1918
Miscellaneous	HQ. 57th Division	05/09/1918	05/09/1918
War Diary	Fampoux Sheet 51B	01/08/1918	09/08/1918
War Diary	Victory Camp	09/08/1918	29/08/1918
War Diary	Casualties Strength Ration	28/08/1918	31/08/1918
Miscellaneous			
Operation(al) Order(s)	8th (Irish) Battn "The King's" (Liverpool Regt) Operation Order No. 43	04/08/1918	04/08/1918
Miscellaneous	8th (Irish) Battn "The King's" (Liverpool Regt)	08/08/1918	08/08/1918
Miscellaneous	8th (Irish) Bn "The King's (L'Pool Regt)	09/03/1918	09/03/1918
Operation(al) Order(s)	8th (Irish) Battn "The King's" (Liverpool Regt) Operation Order No. 44	07/08/1918	07/08/1918
Miscellaneous	Administrative Instruction With Reference To Operation Order 44	07/08/1918	07/08/1918
Miscellaneous	8th (Irish) Battalion "The King's" (L'Pool R.)Administrative Instruction Issued With Provisional Defence Scheme	09/08/1918	09/08/1918
Operation(al) Order(s)	8th (Irish) Battn "The King's" (Liverpool Regiment) Operation Order No. 43	12/08/1918	12/08/1918
Operation(al) Order(s)	8th (Irish) Battn "The King's" (Liverpool Regiment) Operation Order No. 44	14/08/1918	14/08/1918
Miscellaneous	Administrative Instructions Issued In accordance with Operation Order No. 44	14/08/1918	14/08/1918
Heading	8th Liverpool September 1918		

Heading			
	50th Division 1/4th Northumberland Fusrs Vol III Sept 15		
War Diary	Hendecourt Sheet 51.B.U.16	01/09/1918	01/09/1918
War Diary	Sheet 51.B.U.15.B.	04/09/1918	12/09/1918
War Diary	Inchy	13/09/1918	18/09/1918
War Diary	Sombrin	19/09/1918	25/09/1918
War Diary	Queant	27/09/1918	30/09/1918
Miscellaneous		03/09/1918	03/09/1918
Operation(al) Order(s)	8th (Irish) Bn "The King's" (Liverpool Regt) Operation Order No. 47	07/09/1918	07/09/1918
Miscellaneous	Administrative Instructions Issued In Accordance Wit Operation Order No. 47		
Miscellaneous	Provisional Defence Scheme	09/08/1918	09/08/1918
Operation(al) Order(s)	8th (Irish) Battn "The King's" (Liverpool Regt) Operation Order No. 46	17/08/1918	17/08/1918
Miscellaneous	Administrative Instructions Issued In Accordance With Operation Order No. 46	17/08/1918	17/08/1918
Miscellaneous	Preliminary Report On Operations East And South East Of Inchy	11/09/1918	11/09/1918
Miscellaneous	Headquarters 171st Infantry Brigade	11/09/1918	11/09/1918
Miscellaneous	Report On Canal-Du-Nord At A Point 57C N.E.-E.8.d.5.6.		
Miscellaneous	Report on Enemy Operations against Mouevre	12/09/1918	12/09/1918
Miscellaneous	Headquarters 171st Infantry Brigade	14/09/1918	14/09/1918
Operation(al) Order(s)	JOMI Operation Order No. 49	11/09/1918	11/09/1918
Operation(al) Order(s)	8th (Irish) Battn "The King's" (Liverpool Regt) Operation Order No. 51	16/09/1918	16/09/1918
Operation(al) Order(s)	JOMI Operation Order No. 50	11/09/1918	11/09/1918
Operation(al) Order(s)	8th (Irish) Battn "The King's" (Liverpool Regt) Operation Order No. 52	24/09/1918	24/09/1918
Miscellaneous	Administrative Instructions Issued In Accordance With Operation Order No. 52	24/09/1918	24/09/1918
Miscellaneous	8th K.L.R.		
Operation(al) Order(s)	8th (Irish) Battalion "The King's" (Liverpool Regt) Operation Order No. 53	26/09/1918	26/09/1918
Miscellaneous	8th (Irish) Battn. "The King's" (Liverpool Regiment)	25/09/1918	25/09/1918
Miscellaneous	Report On Operation West Of Cambrai	03/10/1918	03/10/1918
Map	Map		
Miscellaneous	Reference Sketch On Back		
Map	Map		
Miscellaneous	Reference Sketch On Back		
War Diary	Proville Sheet 57B N.W.A.20.B	01/10/1918	10/10/1918
War Diary	Boursies	12/10/1918	12/10/1918
War Diary	Haillicourt	14/10/1918	17/10/1918
War Diary	Honnevain	24/10/1918	24/10/1918
War Diary	Rue Franche	25/10/1918	31/10/1918
Miscellaneous	Report On Operations Carried Out From 1st To 9th October 1918		
Map	Map		
Operation(al) Order(s)	8th (Irish) Battn "The King's" (Liverpool Regiment) Operation Order No. 56	04/10/1918	04/10/1918
Miscellaneous	Administrative Instructions With Reference To Operation Order No. 55	04/10/1918	04/10/1918
Miscellaneous	8th KLR O.O.58		
Miscellaneous	Tedo O.O No.57		
Miscellaneous	Tedo Operation Order		

Type	Description	Date From	Date To
Operation(al) Order(s)	8th (Irish) Battn "The King's" (Liverpool Regiment) Operation Order No. 59	11/10/1918	11/10/1918
Operation(al) Order(s)	8th (Irish) Battn "The King's" (Liverpool Regiment) Operation Order No. 60	14/10/1918	14/10/1918
Miscellaneous	Administrative Instructions Issued With Operation Order No. 60	14/10/1918	14/10/1918
Operation(al) Order(s)	8th (Irish) Battn "The King's" (Liverpool Regt) Operation Order No. 61	16/10/1918	16/10/1918
Miscellaneous	Administrative Instructions With Reference To Operation Order 61	16/10/1918	16/10/1918
Operation(al) Order(s)	8th (Irish) Battn "The King's" (Liverpool Regt) Operation Order No. 62	16/10/1918	16/10/1918
Miscellaneous	Administrative Instructions Issued In Accordance With Operation Order No. 62	16/10/1918	16/10/1918
Miscellaneous	Report On Operations Carried Out From 17th To 23rd October 1918	01/11/1918	01/11/1918
Miscellaneous	Special Order By J.P. Johns M.C. Commanding 9th (Irish) Battalion "The King's" (Liverpool Regiment)	21/10/1918	21/10/1918
Miscellaneous	8th (Irish) Battalion The Kings (Liverpool) Regiment	24/10/1918	24/10/1918
Operation(al) Order(s)	8th (Irish) Battalion "The King's" (Liverpool Regt) Operation Order No. 63	29/10/1918	29/10/1918
Miscellaneous	Administrative Instructions Issued In Accordance With Operation Order No. 63	29/10/1918	29/10/1918
War Diary	Hellemes	01/11/1918	01/12/1918
War Diary	Lille	02/12/1918	02/12/1918
War Diary	Carvin	03/12/1918	03/12/1918
War Diary	Arras	04/12/1918	27/12/1918
War Diary	Berneville	29/12/1918	31/12/1918
Operation(al) Order(s)	8th (Irish) Battalion "The King's" (Liverpool Regt) Operation Order No. 64	30/11/1918	30/11/1918
Miscellaneous	Administrative Instructions Issued In Accordance With Operation Order No. 64		
Operation(al) Order(s)	8th (Irish) Battalion "The King's" (Liverpool Regiment) Operation Order No. 65	26/12/1918	26/12/1918
War Diary	Berneville Ref Lens II 3.I.05.22.	01/01/1919	31/01/1919
War Diary	Berneville Map Ref Q.6.d.8.9 Sheet 51.C	01/02/1919	18/03/1919
War Diary	Maroeuil Map Ref L.2.c.4.6 Sheet 51.c	19/03/1919	31/03/1919
Operation(al) Order(s)	8th (Irish) Battalion "The King's" (Liverpool Regiment) Operation Order No. 160	17/03/1919	17/03/1919
Miscellaneous	Headquarters 57th Division	05/05/1919	05/05/1919
War Diary	Maroeuil Map Ref L.2.c.4.6 Sheet 51.c	01/04/1919	30/04/1919
Miscellaneous	Headquarters 57th Division	01/06/1919	01/06/1919
War Diary	Maroeuil Map. Ref L.2.c.4.6 Sheet 57.c	01/05/1919	31/05/1919

WO95/2983/5

57 DIV
171 INFANTRY BDE

1/8 KING'S LIVERPOOL REGT
Feb 1918 – May 1919

57 DIVISION

171 BDE

1/8 KINGS LIVERPOOL REGT

1918 FEB — 1919 MAY

FROM 55 DIV 164 BDE

(ABSORBED 2/8 BN 1918 FEB)

FROM 55 DIV 164 BDE

Box 2983

8th (Irish) Battalion
The Kings Liverpool Regt. WAR DIARY
INTELLIGENCE SUMMARY.

Army Form C. 2118.

Ref map Sheet 36 N.W. (Erase heading not required.)

Place	Date	Hour	Summary of Events and Information	Remarks and references to Appendices
Watou Laudo Camp B.2.C	1st Feby		Re-organization of Battalion. Eff. Strength 52 Officers & 927 OR.	
do	2nd Feby		Relieved 24th Battn. K.L.R in front line & 2 companies of 24th S.L.R in Subsidiary line La Spinette Petit Sector. Company dispositions as follows:- Front Line Right A Coy, Subsidiary Line Right B Coy. do do Left C Coy do Left D Coy	Appendix (1)
	3/4th Feby		Very quiet tour in the line - Casualties 1 wounded	
	5th Feby		Relieved in La Spinette Sector by 24th S.L.R and Battalion moved into billets in Pont-de-Nieppe - Cleaning and reconnaissance of the Houplines Sector by Officers & N.C.O's	Appendix (2)
Pont de Nieppe B.29.b	6/7th Feby		Re-organization of Battalion. 7th Feby Draft of 56 OR arrived.	
do	8th Feby		Relieved 27th K.L.R in Houplines Sector. Infant dispositions as follows:- Front Line Right A Coy, Subsidiary Line Right B Coy do do Left D Coy do Left C Coy	Appendix (3)
	9/10th Feby		Very quiet tour in the line - Casualties 2 OR wounded	

Commanding 8th (Irish) Batt. K.L.R.

8th (Pres) Battalion The King's
Liverpool Regiment

WAR DIARY

INTELLIGENCE SUMMARY.

Army Form C. 2118.

Instructions regarding War Diaries and Intelligence Summaries are contained in F. S. Regs., Part II. and the Staff Manual respectively. Title pages will be prepared in manuscript.

Trench Map Sheet 36 NW (Erase heading not required.)

Place	Date	Hour	Summary of Events and Information	Remarks and references to Appendices
	11th Feby		Relieved in the Houplines Sector by the 2/6th K.L.R. and move into support to Houplines Sector. Disposition of Battalion as follows:- A Coy. Subsidiary Line (centre) C. Coy - Houplines B.& D. Coys at Jute Factory B.29.b. HQ. H.56.80.65.	Appendix (A)
	12/13th		Cleaning reorganisation of Companies	
	14th Feby		Brigade Relief. This Battn was relieved in support to the Houplines Sector by the 14th Battn Welsh Regt and came out into billets at Pont de Nieppe B.23.a.	Appendix (B)
Pont de Nieppe	15th Feby		Cleaning up. Inspection of B & HQ Companies by C.O.	
	16th Feby		Coys under Coy Commanders for Inspection Training	
	17/25th Feby		Working parties of 300 O.R.s per day provided for work on the Corps Line under R.E. supervision	
	26th Feby		Draft of 73 O.R.'s arrived	
	18/23 Feby		Courses for Officers & N.C.O's in the following subjects - Lewis Gun - musketry -	
	25/28 Feby		Drill - Sniping & Observation - Patrolling - carried out under specialist Instructors	
	28 Feby		Off Strength 49 Officers 984 Other Ranks	J.P. Brunskill Major Commanding 8th (Irish) Battn K.L.R.

SECRET.   COPY NO.1.

1/8th (IRISH) BATT. "THE KING'S" (L'POOL R).

OPERATION ORDER NO.1.

Ref: Map Sheet 36 N.W. 1/20,000.
Special Map, 1/10,000 attached.   In the Field.
                                                     1/2/18.

(1) This Battalion will relieve the 2/8th K.L.R. in front
    line and 2 Companies 2/4th S.Lan.R. in subsidiary
    line L'EPINETTE Sub-section to-morrow 2/2/18.

(2) Companies will take over as follows:-

    "A" Company. (plus 1 L.G.Section of "B" Coy).

    Front Line HOUGHTON ROAD, FORT EGAL AVENUE, both
    inclus. occupying posts Nos. 2, 2, 3, 4, 8, 9, 15, 17,
    19. Coy.H.Qrs. HEADQUARTERS' WALK.

    "B" COMPANY. less 1 L.G.Section. (under orders of O.C. "A" Coy)

    3 platoons subsidiary line LOTHIAN AVENUE, FORT EGAL
    AVENUE, both inclus: 2 sections at FORT EGAL FARM.
    2 sections FORT EGAL REDOUBT. Coy.H.Qrs. I.9.b.50.30.

    "C" COMPANY. plus 2 L.G.Sections of "D" Coy.

    Front Line FORT EGAL AVENUE clou: AUSTRALIA AVENUE incl.
    Occupying posts 5, 6, 7, 21, 23, 24, 27, 28, 30, 34,
    and 35.   Coy.H.Qrs. PLANK AVENUE.

    "D" COMPANY. less 2 L.G.Sections under Command of
                                              O.C. "C" Co.
    3 platoons subsidiary line FORT EGAL AVENUE
    exclus: C.28.c.60.95. one platoon QUALITY STREET
    Coy.H.Qrs. I.4.a.55.80.

(3) 2/9th Bn.K.L.R. will arrange for one guide per post
    to be occupied vide para.2 to rendezvous at 4.45 p.m.
    at SQUARE FARM.
    Advance Officers of subsidiary line Companies will
    make arrangements they may require with Company to be
    relieved.

(4) Lewis Guns will precede the Battalion, leaving
    WATERLANDS CAMP at 1 p.m. Limbers to be at Camp
    at 12.45 p.m. Lewis Gun Officer will arrange for
    guides to meet teams at SQUARE FARM and conduct them
    to POSTS after drawing gum boots.

(5) Companies will move off from WATERLANDS CAMP as
    under:-
                "C" Company...... 3 p.m.
                "A"   "   ....3.15 "
                "D"   "   ....3.30 "
                "B"   "   ....3.45 p.m.
                H.Qrs.   ....4 p.m.

(6) Companies will move via ERQUINGHEM 100 yards distance
    between platoons.

(7) One Officer, one L.G. N.C.O. and one Runner will
    per Company will proceed to the line to-morrow at
    9.30 a.m. and make a reconnaissance of sectors to be
    occupied.

(8) Trench Stores, work in hand, and that contemplated
    to be taken over on relief.

SECRET.

-2-

(9) Completion of relief will be reported by wire "BABY".

(10) Administrative Instructions have been issued to all concerned.

(11) ACKNOWLEDGE.

Issued at 9.30 p.m.
By Runner.
Copies to:-
1. 171 Inf. Bde.
2. C.O.
3. 2nd-in-Command.
4. O.C. "A" Coy.
5. " "B" "
6. " "C" "
7. " " "
8. " H.Qrs. Details.
9. L.G.O.
10. Sig. Off.
11. Transport Off.
12. 2/9th K.L.R.
13. Q.M.
14. M.O.
15. R.S.M.
16. Intell. Off.
17. File.
18. War Diary.

W. Hornby
2/Lt.
for Capt. & Adjt.
1/8th (Irish) Batt. K.L.R.

-o-o-o-o-o-o-o-o-o-o-o-o-o-

SECRET.   COPY NO....

8th (IRISH) BATTALION "THE KING'S" (L'POOL REGIMENT).

Administrative Instructions
with reference to O.O. No.1.
-------------------o-------------------

In the Field.
1/2/18.

(1) KIT FOR TRENCHES. Officers' Trench Kit, Company Stores etc. will be ready at Company H.Qrs. for removal by 2.30 p.m.

(2) DRESS. One blanket per man will be carried - leather jerkins being worn, greatcoats in valises. P.H. Helmets will not be worn but will be collected and stored under Company arrangements.

(3) SURPLUS KITS ETC. Surplus Kits, Blankets neatly rolled in bundles of 10 and labelled, stores etc. will be stacked in huts now occupied by Signal Section. Huts to be clear of latter by 2.15 p.m.

(4) GUM BOOTS. Companies taking over front line will draw gum boots at SQUARE FARM before moving up.
No gum boots will be taken over in the line.

W. Hornby
2/Lieut.
for Capt. & Adjt.
1/8th (Irish) Battalion K.L.R.

Issued at 9.45 p.m.

SECRET.   Copy No......
8th (IRISH) BATTN. "THE KING'S" (L'POOL REGT.)

OPERATION ORDER NO.2.

Ref. Map sheet 36. N.W.   In the Field.
1/20,000.   5.2.18.
----

1. The 8th. K.L.R. will be relieved by 2/4th. S. Lancs. Regt.,
   in L'EPINETTE SECTOR on night 5th Feb. 1918.

2. After relief 8th. K.L.R. will move to PONT-de-NIEPPE.

2. Guides will be supplied by this Unit as under:-
   (a) 1 per L.G. Team to be at SQUARE FARM at 3.15p.m.
   (b) 1 per Coy. to be at SANDBAG CORNER at 4.15p.m.
   (c) 1 per Post from Front Line Coys. 1 per Counter-attack
       Platoon and Section. 1 per Platoon in Subs. Line.
       To be at SQUARE FARM at 4.45p.m.
   Guides will be in possession of chits showing Posts to which
   they are guiding incoming Unit.

3. Work in hand and that contemplated will be carefully handed
   over.

4. Receipts will be obtained for all Trench Stores handed over,
   and one copy to be forwarded to B.H.Q. by 9a.m. 6.2.18.

5. Lieut. E.J. Woodcock. will report to B.H.Q., 2/4th S.L.Regt.,
   and take over stores and arrange for billets etc.

6. Relief complete will be wired by code words as under :-
       "A" Coy. BARBED.   "B" WIRE.
       "C" "   SCREW.   "D" PICKETS.

7. Administrative Instructions have been issued to all concerned.

8. ACKNOWLEDGE.

                                        W. Hornby
                                        2/Lt. & Actg. Adjt.,
Issued at 11a.m.   8th (Irish) Bn. K.L.R.
By Runner.
Copies to:-
    No.1. C.O.   2. 2nd in Cd.   3. O.C. "A" Coy.
    4. O.C. "B" Coy.   5. O.C. "C" Coy.   6.   " "D" "
    7. H.Q. Details.   8. Transport Off.   9. Q.M.
    10 2/4th. S.L.R. 11. L.G.O.   12. R.S.M.
    13 War Diary.   14. File.
    -------------------oOo-------------------

SECRET.   Copy. No.....
8th (IRISH) BATTN. "THE KING'S" (L'POOL REGT.)

            Administrative Instructions   In the Field.
            with reference to O.O. No.2.   5.2.18.
            ....

1. Officers' Trench Kits, Coy. Stores etc. will be stacked under
   Coy. Loading Parties at Ration Dumps by 6p.m.

2. L.G. Limbers will be at SQUARE FARM at 7p.m.

3. All Gum Boots will be returned to SQUARE FARM on relief.

4. O.C. Coys. will ensure that their Sectors are handed over in
   a clean and sanitary condition.

                                        W. Hornby
                                        2/Lt. & Actg. Adjt.,
                                        8th (Irish) Bn. K.L.R.

Issued at 11a.m.

Operation Order No. 3. 8th (Irish) Bn. K.L.R.
                    Sheet No. 2.
                        .....

Issued at ..7.30. p.m.
By RUNNER.

Copies to
   1. C.O.   10. L.G.O.
   2. 2nd in Command.   11. Sig. Officer.
   3. O.C. "A" Coy.   12. T.O.
   4. O.C. "B" "   13. 2/7th K.L.R.
   5. " "C" "   14. Quartermaster.
   6. " "D" "   15. M.O.
   7. " H.Q. Details.   16. R.S.M.
   8. " 2/7th K.L.R.)   17. War Diary.
          Counter Attack Coy.)   18. File.
   9. Intelligence Offr.   19. War Diary.

                        ....

SECRET. COPY No. .....

8th (Irish) Bn. "The King's" Liverpool Regt.

Ref. Map.
Sheet 36 N7.   OPERATION ORDER NO. 3.   In the Field.
1/20,000.   ......   7.2.1918.

(1) This Battalion will relieve the 2/7th Bn. K.L.R. in HOUPLINES Sub-Sector tomorrow 8.2.1918.

(2) Coys. will take over as below:-

"D" Coy. (plus one L.G. Section from "A" Coy) - Front Line, Right Sector, Brigade Boundary C.29.c.2.6 to WESSEX AVENUE (exclusive) occupying Posts Nos. 1, 2, 3, 8, 9, 10, 11, 12, 15, and 2 Sections FRY PAN, and 2 Sections right of SPAIN AVENUE. Coy. H.Q. GLOUCESTER AVENUE.

"B" Coy. (plus one L.G. Section from "C" Coy) will take over Front Line from WESSEX AVENUE (inclusive) to RIVER LYS, occupying Posts Nos. 4, 5, 16, 18, 20, 25, 26, 27, 28, L.G. Post in PETERS CUT, Night Post right of CAMBRIDGE AVENUE, two sections left of SUSSEX AVENUE and two sections left of PANAMA CANAL. Coy. H.Q. right of SUSSEX AVENUE.

"A" Coy. - Right Subsidiary Coy.

"C" Coy. - Left Subsidiary Coy.

One Coy. Support Battn. - Centre Subsidiary Coy.
(2/5th K.L.R.)

(3) 2/7th K.L.R. will arrange for one guide per post to be occupied vide Para. 2 to rendezvous at 4.45 p.m. at HOUPLINES LEVEL CROSSING C.27.a.2.1.

(4) Advance Party of L.G. Officer and one L.G. N.C.O. and one Officer and 2 N.C.Os. per Coy. will report to Coys. they are relieving by 11.30 a.m.

(5) Lewis Gun Teams will precede the Battalion. Guides will meet them at TISSAGE DUMP at 3.30 p.m. and conduct them to Posts after drawing Gum boots.

(6) Coys. will move off from PONT DE NIEPPE as under -
"B" Coy.   4.0 p.m.
"D" "   4.15
"C" "   4.30
"A" "   2.25
H.Q.   5.0

(7) Coys. will move in file.   Platoons at 100 yds distance.

(8) Trench Stores, Maps, Defence Schemes, work in hand and that contemplated will be taken over on relief.

(9) Completion of relief will be signalled -
"A" Coy. LOFTY.   "B" Coy. CARBON.
"C" "   BARR.   "D" "   HARRY.
Counter Attack Coy. (2/7th K.L.R.)- O.C. Coy. will report personally to Bn. H.Q.

(10) Administrative instructions have been issued to all concerned.

(11) ACKNOWLEDGE.

R.J.Bordwick

Lieut. and Asst. Adjt.,

SECRET.   COPY NO. 15

8th (IRISH) BATTALION "THE KING'S" (L'POOL R).
Operation Order No. 4

Ref: Sheet 36 N.W. Edit.8A., 1/20.000.
Trench Map.
                                                                                 In the Field.
                                                                                 10/2/18.

(1) This Battalion will be relieved in the HOUPLINES SECTOR by the 2/6th L'Pool R. on the night 11/2/18.

(2) Companies will be relieved as hereunder:-
   "D" Coy. in Right Front Coy.Subsector by "B" Coy.2/6th K.L.R.
   "B" " " Left   "   "   " "A" " "   "
   "A" " " Right Subsid.Coy. "   " "C" " "   "
   "C" " " Left   "   "   " "D" " "   "

(3) One guide for each post will report to HOUPLINES LEVEL CROSSING N C.27.a.90.15. to meet incoming unit at 4.30 p.m. Each guide will be furnished with a note shewing Post to which he is detailed to guide the relief.

(4)(a) On relief, Companies will move to the following positions :-
   Headquarters: H.5.b.90.60.
   "A" Company C Will become Centre Subsidiary Company, HOUPLINES SECTOR and will come under orders of O.C. 2/6th K.L.R. reporting personally to O.C. 2/6th K.L.R. when in position.
   "C" Company : HOUPLINES.
   "B" & "D" Companies : JUTE FACTORY.
   (b) Capt.H.S.WILSON will report at 12 noon 11/2/18 to O.C. 2/7th K.L.R. at H.5.b.90.89 and take over billets stores etc. A guide from 2/7th K.L.R. will report to O.C. "C" Company at 10 a.m. 11/2/18 for the purpose of guiding one man per platoon to billets at HOUPLINES.
   These guides will meet the Company on relief at junction of Wessex Avenue and Tramline.

(5) Particulars of all work in progress and proposed will be carefully handed over to incoming unit. Trench stores will be carefully handed over and receipts taken : these will be forwarded to Battalion H.Q. not later than 12 Noon 12/2/18.

(6) Completion of reliefs will be signalled: the following Code words being used:-

     "A" Coy. JAN.   "B" Coy. FEB.
     "C" "   MAR.   "D" "   APR.

(7) Batt.H.Q. will close at HOUPLINES SECTOR at 8 p.m. and will open at H.5.b.90.60. at that time.

(8) Administrative instructions have been issued to all concerned.

A C K N O W L E D G E.

                                                                  Capt. & Adjt.
                                                   8th (Irish) Battalion K.L.R.

Issued at 8 p.m.
  Copies to:-
      see over.

1. 171 Inf.Bde.
2. C.O.
3. 2nd in Command.
4. Adjutant.
5. O.C. 2/6th K.L.R.
6. O/C entre S&Bsid.Coy. 2/7th K.L.R.
7. Intell.Off.
8. Sigs.Off.
9. O.C. "A" Coy.
10. " "B" "
11. " "C" "
12. " "D" "
13. T.O.
14. Q.M.
15. R.S.M.
16. M.O.
17. File.
18. War Diary.

SECRET.   8th(Irish)Battalion "The King's"(L'Pool R).

Adminstrative Instructions with
reference to Operation Order No.4.
----

1. Officers' Kits, Company Stores, etc. will be stacked at
   TISSAGE DUMP in charge of Company Loading Parties by
   6.30 p.m.

2. Transport Officer will arrange for limbers to be at
   TISSAGE DUMP by 6.30 p.m.

3. All Gum Boots will be returned to Gum Boot Stores, TISSAGE
   DUMP.   No Gum Boots will be handed over in the line.

4. O.C.Companies will ensure that their sections are handed
   over in a clean and sanitary condition, receipts to this
   effect being obtained from incoming Unit.

                                    [signature]
                                    Capt. & Adjt.
                                    8th(Irish)Battalion K.L.R.

Issued at 9.45 p.m.
To all concerned.

SECRET.

8th (IRISH) BATTALION "THE KING'S (LIVERPOOL REGT.)"

OPERATION ORDER No.5.

Ref: Map 5 N.W. 1/20000.

In the Field.
14/2/18.

(1) This Battalion will be relieved in the HOUPLINES SUPPORT sector by the 14th Battalion Welsh R. on the night 14/15th Feb. 1918.

(2)(a) Companies will be relieved as hereunder:-

"A" Coy in Subsidiary line (centre) by C Coy. "Welsh"
"C" " Houplines " D " " "
B & D Companies in Jute Factory " A & B Coys. "Welsh"

(b) Relief of Battalion H.Q. and B & D Companies will commence about 3 p.m. 14th Feb. 1918. A & C Companies will not move from their respective subsectors until 2/6th K.L.R. have been relieved.

(c) East of River LYS movement will be by platoons at 100 yards distance - West of River LYS 100 yards between Companies.

(3) On relief Companies will proceed to billets at PONT DE NIEPPE. O.C. Companies will report personally when their commands are settled in billets.

(4) Billets at PONT DE NIEPPE will be taken over by Capt.H.S. WILSON. One N.C.O. per Company will report to him at Q.M.Stores at 10 a.m. 14/2/18.

(5) All Defence Schemes and other papers referring to the sector will be handed over on relief and receipts taken.
Particulars of all work in progress and proposed will be handed over in detail. Trench Stores will be carefully handed over and receipts taken. All receipts will be forwarded to Batt.H.Q. by 10.30 a.m. 15/2/18.

(6) Batt.H.Q. will close at ERQUINGHEM at 5 p.m. 14/2/18 and will open at PONT DE NIEPPE at that time.

Administrative Instructions have been issued to all concerned.

ACKNOWLEDGE.

J.F. Jones
Capt. & Adjt.
8th(Irish)Batt.K.L.R.

Issued at 11 p.m.

Copies to:-
1. 171 Inf.Bde.
2. C.O.
3. 2nd in Command.
4. 14th Batt.Welsh R.
6. 2/6th K.L.R.
7. Intell.Off.
8. Signalling Off.
9. Patrol Off.
10. O.C. A Coy.
11. O.C. B Coy.
12. O.C. C Coy.
12. O.C. D Coy.
13. Transport Off.
14. Quartermaster.
15. Capt.WILSON.
16. R.S.M.
17. War Diary.
18. File.
19.
20.

8th (Irish) Batt" The Kings (Liverpool Regt)

WAR DIARY
or
INTELLIGENCE SUMMARY.

Army Form C. 2118.

March 1918

Place	Date	Hour	Summary of Events and Information	Remarks and references to Appendices
1918 March				
Nœux	1st		Battalion strength 49 Officers 914 other ranks.	Yes
			Nor 96 Batt. H.Q. continued Bath embarking HAVERSKERQUE Camphor	Yes
			moving to … mine site	
Bossey	2nd & 3rd		Training Special orders were issued to Trainers. Lewis Gun Classes, Snipers v Scouts, Companies & Bren Groups Lewis Guns every day	Yes
	10th		Rake/Drive orders Battalion entrained at BEUVRY 8 a.m on arrival at CAUDESCURE now MERVILLE Usual duties & worked two	Yes
	11th		divisions	
			Short field Exercise by Divisions & Brigades held. LAVENTIE —	Yes
Caudescure	12th		Brigade exercise recommenced	
			Short field Exercise Brigade Groups held near NEUVE CHAPELLE	
	13th		recommenced	
	14th		Inspection of Battalion by Lt. J.C.E.	Yes
	15th		Training Kaher Ready. Raining all day	Yes
	16th		Training Kaher Gun & Pistol	Yes
			MERVILLE Relieved about noon.	Yes

O.T. Hall
Lieut. Col Commanding 8th (Irish) Battn K.L.R.

8th (Irish) Batt. "The King's" Liverpool Regiment

Army Form C. 2118.

WAR DIARY
INTELLIGENCE SUMMARY.
(Erase heading not required.)

March 1918   Vol 14

Place	Date	Hour	Summary of Events and Information	Remarks and references to Appendices
Cuinchy	17 March		Church Parade — Firing on 30 yds range — Lieut. Col. E. B. Heath D.S.O. having proceeded on a course the command of the Battn was assumed by Capt. J.F. Jones M.C.	
to	18/20		Training (Musketry, L.G. Classes, Firing on Range 90)	
	21		Moved to Nouveau Monde 36 N.W. G.27.c. relieving 5th Battn Berks Regt. as Right Battn Divisional Reserve. Battn routine reconnoitred. Lieut. Col. E. B. Heath D.S.O. having returned from course assumed command of the Battn. Capt J.F. Jones M.C. resumed the duties of 2nd in Command.	(1) A.C.
Nouveau Monde	22/25		Training (Musketry, Gas Drill, Arm Drill 90)	
	26		Moved to Wurtras Area as Reserve Battn relieving 24th to N Lancs Regt.	(2) A.C.
	27-28		Training (Musketry, L.G. Classes, Physical, Bayonet Fighting)	(3) A.C.
Wurtras 36 N.W. H.36	29		Moved into line as Right Battn in the Bois Grenier Sector relieving 26th Rifle Battn K.R.R.	
			Batt. H.Q. Rye Farm F.36.N.W.4 H.36.a.20.15 Company dispositions as follows:—	
			Right Front D Left Front C } Quiet tour — Enemy artillery active	
			Support B Support A } on rear lines	
			Casualties 1 Off + 3 O.R. missing 1 O.R. Killed 7 O.R.s wounded	
			Strength 32 Off 841 O.R.	H [signature]
	31			E.B. Heath
			Lieut. Col. Commdg. 8th (Irish) Battn K.L.R.	

SECRET.   COPY NO...
            8th (IRISH) BATTALION "THE KING'S" (L'POOL REGT).
                        OPERATION ORDER NO. 9.
                        -o-o-o-o-o-o-o-o-o-o-

Ref: Map HAZEBROUCK 5A, 1/100,000.   20/3/18.

    (1) This Battalion will relieve the 5th Bn. Berks Regt.
        as Right Battn. Divisional Reserve on 21/3/18, at
        NOUVEAU MONDE, moving by March Route.

    (2) Order of March will be:-
        HQrs Company.
        "A"   "
        "B"   "
        "C"   "
        "D"   "
    moving at distances of 100 yards between Coys. Head
    of column will pass point on road directly below T.
    in VERTE RUE at 7.15 a.m.

    (3) Transport will move 100 yards in rear of Battalion
        (less Lewis Gun Limbers).

    (4) Relief complete will be reported by Company Commanders
        in person.

    (5) Defence Scheme, Maps, Stores etc. will be carefully
        taken over, lists being forwarded to Batt. HQrs. by
        6 p.m. 21/3/18.
        Company Commanders will at once reconnoitre their
        Battle positions as per map attached, and will report
        immediately this has been done.

    (6) Battn. HQrs. will close at CAUDESCURE at 7 a.m. and
        reopen at NOUVEAU MONDE at 9 a.m. 21/3/18.

    (7) Administrative Instructions have been issued to all
        concerned.

    A C K N O W L E D G E.

Issued at 3.30 p.m.
Copies to:-
1. 171st Inf. Bde.
2. 5th Bn. Berks R.   Lieut. & A/Adjt.
3. C.O.   8th (Irish) Batt. K.L.R.
4. Adjutant.
5. O.C. HQ Company.
6. Sigs. Off.
7. Intell. Off.
8. L.G.O.
9. O.C. "A" Coy.
10. "   "B" "
11. "   "C" "
12. "   "D" "
13. M.O.
14. T.O.
15. Q.M.
16. RSM.
17. File.
18. War Diary.
19.
20.
21.

-o-o-o-o-o-----o-o-o-o-o-o-

SECRET. COPY NO.

8th (IRISH) BATTALION "THE KING'S" (L'POOL REGIMENT).

Adminstrative Instructions
with reference to Operation Orders No. 9.
-o-o-o-o-o-o-o-o-o-o-o-o-o-o-o-o-o-o-o-o-o-

20/3/18.

(1) Advance Party of one N.C.O. per Company will report to Batt. HQrs. at 8.30 a.m. 20/3/18 and proceed to NOUVEAU MONDE as Billeting Party.

(2) Officers' Valises, all Blankets (neatly rolled in bundles of 10 and labelled), Company Stores etc. will be stacked outside Company HQrs. by 6.30 a.m. 21/3/18.

(3) O.C. Companies will detail one N.C.O. and 2 men as Loading party.
    The Quartermaster will proceed in charge of motor lorries and ensure that all stores are removed.

(4) DRESS : Full Marching Order.

(5) CLEANLINESS: Billets will be left in a scrupulously clean and sanitary condition, and will be ready for inspection by Major T.L. BAILES at 6.30 a.m. A receipt to this effect, in duplicate will be obtained from either the incoming Unit or the Billet Warden and will be rendered to Batt. HQ. by 6 p.m. 21/3/18.

(6) The Medical Officer will arrange to inspect feet of men during the afternoon of 21/3/18.

(7) The Transport Officer will arrange to dump Mobilisation Ammunition at Batt. HQrs. NOUVEAU MONDE.

(8) Attention of all concerned is directed to Circ. Memo. No. 11. "MARCH DISCIPLINE".

ACKNOWLEDGE.

E.W.Woodcock
Lieut. & A/Adjt.
8th (Irish) Battalion K.L.R.

Issued at 4.15 p.m.
Copies to:-
1. C.O.
2. Adjutant.
3. HQ Coy.
4. "A" "
5. "B" "
6. "C" "
7. "D" "
8. Intell. Off.
9. L.G.O.
10. QM.
11. M.O.
12. T.O.
13. RSM.
14. File.
15. War Diary.
16.
17.
18.

SECRET. COPY NO. 5

8th (IRISH) BATTALION "THE KING'S" (LIVERPOOL REGT).

OPERATION ORDER NO. 10

Map Ref. CROIX DU BAC. 1/20,000. 25/3/18.

(1) This Unit will relieve the 2/4th L.N.Lancs.R. as Reserve Battalion in FLEURBAIX AREA to-morrow the 26/3/18.

(2) 2/Lt. O.P. CASEY, one Officer per Company, and one Signallers from HQrs. and one per Company will report to HQrs. of 2/4th L.N.Lan.R. and the respective Coys. to be relieved, at 11 a.m. 26/3/18 to take over.

(3) Companies will relieve as follows:-
                                                                            HQrs.
"A" Coy. will relieve "A" Coy. 2/4th L.N.Lan. H.21.a.1.2.
"B" "   "   "B" "   "   "   "   H.10.a.2.2.
"C" "   "   "C" "   "   "   "   H.17.d.2.1.
"D" "   "   "D" "   "   "   "   H.21.a.1.2.

(4) Companies will move from billets at times stated below, following ESTAIRES - SAILLY ROAD:-
    "A" Coy......... 7.30 p.m.
    "B" " .... 7.35 "
    "C" " .... 7.40 "
    "D" " 7.45
    HQrs. .... 7.50 p
Lewis Gun Limbers and Field Kitchens will proceed with Companies. Movement will be by Platoons at 100 yards Distance.
    O.C. Companies will guide their Companies to their billets. Railway Crossing H.13.c.6 & 30. will not be passed before 3.30 p.m.

(5) "C" Company will provide two A.A. Guns as below. Guide for these will be supplied by O.C. "C" Coy. 2/4th L.N.Lan.R at Coy. HQrs.
    1 Gun.... H.22.a.6.3.
    1 "   .... H.27.b.4.7.

(6) All Maps, Defence Schemes, Log Book, etc.etc. will be carefully taken over and receipts given. Copies of these receipts will reach Batt.HQ. by 9 a.m. 27/3/18.

(7) Relief Complete will be signalled from "B" and "C" Coys. by the Code word "JOHN" - HQrs. "A" and "D" Coys. will report in person.

(8) Battn.HQ. will close at NOUVEAU MONDE at 7.30 p.m. and will open at that time at H.21.a.3.2.

(9) Regt. Aid Post will be at Bn.Hqrs. H.21.a.3.2.

ACKNOWLEDGE.

                                                          E. Woodcock
Issued at 9 p.m.
Copies to:-   Lieut. & A/Adjt.
  1 - 171 Inf. Bde.   7. Intell. Off.   8th (Irish) Battalion K.L.R.
  2. 2/4th L.N.Lan.R. 8. "A" Coy.   14. T.O.
  3. O.C.   9. "B" "   15. Q.M.   19.....
  4. 2nd in Commd.   10. "C" "   16. R.S.M.   20.....
  5. Adjutant.   12. "D" "   17. File.   21.....
  6. O.C. Signallers. 13. M.O.   18. War Diary.   22.....

SECRET.

8th (IRISH) BATTALION "THE KING'S" (L'POOL REGIMENT).   COPY NO....

Administrative Instructions
with reference to Operation Order
No. 10.

"-O-O-O-O-O-O-O-O-O-O-O-O-O-"

25/3/18.

(1) All Surplus Stores, one blanket per man (neatly rolled in bundles of 10 and labelled) will be stacked outside Coy. HQrs. by 9 a.m. 26/3/17 ready for removal. Mobilisation Ammunition on charge of Coys. will be returned to Battn. Dump by 2 p.m. Officers' Kit, Coy. Stores for trenches etc. will be stacked outside Coy. HQ. by 6.30 p.m. 26/3/18.

(2) Transport Officer will arrange to collect Surplus Stores at 9 a.m. (Mobilisation Ammunition at 2.30 p.m.) and return them to Q.M. Stores, and also to collect stores for trenches at 7 p.m. and convey it to respective Coy. HQrs.

(3) DRESS: Leather Jerkins will be worn, overcoat carried in pack, and one blanket carried on pack in ground sheet.

Sd. on Hughes   26/7/14
Lieut. & A/Adjt.
8th (Irish) Batt. K. L. R.

Issued at 9 p.m.
TO ALL CONCERNED.

"-O-O-O-O-O-O-O-O-O-O-"

SECRET.   COPY NO.
           8th (IRISH) BATTALION   THE KING'S (L'POOL REGT).
           -o-o-o-o-o-o-o-o-   -o-o-o-o-o-o-o-o-o-o-

                        OPERATION ORDER NO. 11

Ref: Sheet 36 N.W. 1/20,000.   28/3/18.

(1) This Unit will relieve the 2/6th (Rifle) Bn. K.L.R. as
    Right Battn. in the BOIS GRENIER Sector on the night 29/30th
    March 1918.

(2) Dispositions of Companies will be as follows:-
        BATTALION HEADQUARTERS............ WYE FARM.
        RIGHT FRONT COY. "D" Coy relieving "D" Coy 2/6th K.L.R.
        LEFT   "   "   "B" "   "   "C" "   "
        RIGHT REAR "   "C" "   "   "B" "   "
        LEFT   "   "   "A" "   "   "A" "   "

        Companies will leave billets as under:-
            "D", "C" and "B" Coys...... 7.45 p.m.
            "A" Coy...................   8 p.m.
            HQrs. Coy.................   8.15 p.m.

(3) Lewis Guns will be relieved by daylight. Guides will be
    provided by O.C. 2/6th K.L.R. one per post, as under. Each
    guide will carry a chit shewing position to be occupied.
    24 magazines per gun will be carried.
            "D" Coy   ELBOW FARM...   3 p.m.
            "A" "   do   3.15 p.m.
            "B" "   3.30 p.m.
            "C" "   CROMBALOT DUMP 3 p.m.
                     (H.30.a.5.3.)
    Remainder of magazines and boxes will be taken by Transport
    to Dumps and sent down to posts immediately on arrival.
    Teams will move at a distance of 200 yards.

(4) Guides for Companies and HQrs. will rendezvous as follows:-
        1 Guide per Post and Coy. HQrs. and one Guide for Battn. HQrs.
            "D" Coy.......... ELBOW FARM... 8 p.m.
            "B" "...........   do   do.
            "A" "...........   do   do.
            "C" "........... CROMBALOT DUMP 8 p.m.
                              (H.30.a.5.3.)
            HQrs............. ELBOW FARM... 8 p.m.
    Each guide will bear a chit shewing position to be taken over.
    Movement will be by platoons in file at 200 yards distance.

(5) Advance party of 2/Lt H. CHESHIRE, one Officer per Coy.
    R.S.M., 2 Signallers from HQrs. and 2 per Coy will proceed to
    Battn. HQ. WYE FARM and to Companies by 2 p.m. to take over
    stores etc.

(6) Defence Schemes, Maps, Trench Stores etc. will be carefully
    taken over and receipts given, copies of which will be
    forwarded to Battn. HQ. by 8.30 a.m. 30/3/18.

(7) Relief Complete will be signalled "ROAD".

(8) Administrative Instructions have been issued to all concerned.
        ACKNOWLEDGE.
                                              E.J. Dooley
Issued at 8.30 p.m.   Lieut. & A/Adjt.
Copies to:-   8th (Irish) Batt. K.L.R.
    1. 171 Inf. Bde.   7. Intell. Off.   13. "D" Coy.   20.
    2. 2/6th K.L.R.   8. L.G.O.   14. M.O.   21.
    3. O.C.   9. Patrol Off.   15. T.O.   22.
    4. 2nd in Command. 10. "A" Coy.   16. Q.M.
    5. Adjutant.   11. "B" "   17. R.S.M.
    6. Signals Off.   12. "C" "   18. File.
                                          19. War Diary.

SECRET.   COPY NO.

8th (IRISH) BATTALION "THE KING'S" (L'POOL REGT)

Administrative Instructions with reference to Opern. Order No. 11.

-o-o-o-o-o-o-o-o-o-o-o-o-o-o-o-o-o-o-o-o-

                                                           /3/18.

(1) All Officers' Trench Kits, Company Stores, L.G. Magazines etc. will be stacked ready for removal at Coy. HQ. by 8.30 p.m. 29/3/18. 1 N.C.O. and 3 men per limber will be detailed as loading party.

(2) Receipts for Stores handed over and cleanliness certificates will be obtained from incoming Unit 2/6th (Rifle) Bn. K.L.R. and forwarded to Batt. HQ. by 8.30 a.m. 30/3/18. Billet of "B" Coy will not be taken over.

(3) O.C. "C" and "A" Companies will each detail a guide from their A.A. position to report to Battn HQ by 11 a.m. 29/3/18 to conduct No. 1 of relieving team to position. These guns will be dismounted and not wait for relieving guns.

(4) Transport Officer will arrange to collect HQ. and Coy. Stores, L.G. Mags. etc. and dump them as below:-

    "D" Company ...... GUNNERS WALK.
    "C"   "   ...... GREATWOOD AVENUE.
    "B"   "   ...... ELBOW FARM.
    "A"   "   ...... COMMAND POST.

Cookers will be returned to Transport Lines.

(5) DRESS - FULL MARCHING ORDER. Leather Jerkins will be worn. Greatcoats in Pack and one blanket folded in Ground Sheet.

(6) Regimental Aid Post will be at TEMPLE H.36.a.6.0.

                                                   Lieut. & A/Adjt.
                                       8th (Irish) Battalion K.L.R.

Issued at 8.30 p.m.
Copies to:-
1. C.O.
2. 2nd in Command.
3. Adjutant.
4. Signalling Off.
5. Intell. Off. & L.G.O.
6. Patrolling Off.
7. "A" Coy.
8. "B" "
9. "C" "
10. "D" "
11. M.O.
12. T.O.
13. Q.M.
14. R.S.M.
15. File.
16. War Diary.

57th Division.
171st Infantry Bde.

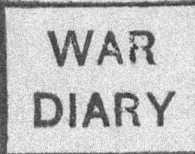

8th BATTALION

THE KING'S LIVERPOOL REGIMENT

APRIL 1918

SECRET.
Headquarters,
    57th Division.

    Herewith War Diary for this Battalion for the month of April 1918.

                                      Lieut.-Colonel,
                Commdg. 8th (Irish) Bn. K. L. R.

1.5.18.

Army Form C. 2118.

8th (Irish) Batt: "The King's" Liverpool Regiment

WAR DIARY
INTELLIGENCE SUMMARY.

April 1918.

Sheet No 1.   (Erase heading not required.)

Place	Date	Hour	Summary of Events and Information	Remarks and references to Appendices
Plouvain	1/4/18		Strength 32 Officers 841 Other Ranks. Relieved in right sub-sector Bois Grenier Sector by 12th Battr Suffolk Regt. Casualties 1.O.R. killed 1.O.R. wounded. Moved into hutments at Estaires.	1.
Estaires	2/4/18		Entrained and arrived at Doullens at mid-day 3/4/18	2.
Le Souich	4/4/18		Marched to Frévillers. Marched to billets at Le Souich. Refixing 11. H.E.	
Warlincourt	5&6/4/18		Marched to billets at Warlincourt Ry Line 11. 4. G. Batln under one hour's notice to move between 8.0 am - 12 noon 3 hours notice for remainder of each day	
	5&6/4/18		Cleaning up. Training (Musketry, Physical Drill, Arms Drill, ?@)	
	7/4/18		Reconnaissance of forward areas by HQ Officers & Coy Commanders. On return of Major J.H. Bowring from leave Capt. G. Jones M.C. resumed the position of Adjutant.	
	8/4/18		Marched to billets at Terramesnil Ref Line 11.5.E. Under one hour's notice to move all day.	3.
	9/10/4/18		Reconnaissance of forward areas by HQ Officers & Coy Commanders. Training (Physical & Arms Drill, musketry ?@)	
	11/4/18		Training (Physical - Arms Drill, musketry ?@). Major C.B. Schüss arrived on 10th Batr. took over Command of O Company from 11th April.	

Lieut. Col. Comndg. 8th (Irish) Battn. King's Pool Regt.

A6945. Wt.W17422/M1180 350000 12/16 D.D.&L. Forms/C/2118/14

8th (Irish) Batt. The Kings Regiment
Liverpool Regiment

WAR DIARY
INTELLIGENCE SUMMARY

Army Form C. 2118.

Sheet No. 2.

Place	Date	Hour	Summary of Events and Information	Remarks and references to Appendices
Tenancourt	12/4/18		Marched to POMMERA	
Pommera	13/4/18		Marched to Camp South of AUTUIE by Rens 11. S.F. under one hours notice to move.	④
Autuie	14-15-16/4/18		Orders for manning rcd lines in event of enemy attack. Reconnaissance of positions by Officers	
	16/4/18		Marched to Camp East of PAS by Rens 11. S.G.	⑤ & 6 ⑦
Pas.	17/4/18		Batt⁰ on working party in Red line East of Souastre ready for immediate defence. Lewis Gun Classes	
	18/4/18		Training in Camp (Firing on Range, musketry, Lewis Gun, Squad Drill)	
		21.23.26	Batt⁰ on Working Party in line East of Souastre, ready for immediate defence. Lewis Gun Classes	
		27,29 Apl		
		22,24,26,28,30 Apl	Training in Camp (Firing on Range, musketry, Lewis Gun, Squad Arm Drill)	
			Orders for manning of line in event of enemy attack - Reconnaissance by Officers	⑧
			Strength 37 Officers & 960 Other Ranks	

J. H. Collins
Lieut Colonel Commdg
8th (Irish) Batt⁰ Kings Liverpool Regt

SECRET. COPY NO...

8th (IRISH) BATT. "THE KING'S" (L'POOL REGIMENT).

OPERATION ORDER NO. 12.

Ref: Maps, HAZEBROUCK 5A, 1/100,000.
36 N.W. 1/20,000.   1/4/18.

(1) This Battalion will be relieved by the 12th Battn. Suffolk Regt. in the Right Bn. Sub-Sector, BOIS GRENIER Sector, on the night of 1/2nd April, 1918.

(2) Companies of 12th Bn. Suffolk R. will take over from this Unit as under:-

"A" Coy. 12th Suffolks. from "D" Coy. RIGHT FRONT.
"B"   "   "   "   "C" "   LEFT   "
"C"   "   "   "   "B" "   RIGHT SUPPORT
"D"   "   "   "   "A" "   LEFT   "

(3) <u>GUIDES</u>. Guides for incoming Unit will be supplied as under:-

One Guide from Batt. HQ. and one per Coy. to meet CQMSs. at ELBOW FARM at 3 p.m. 1/4/18, and will conduct the CQMSs. to their respective Company Ration Dumps.

One Guide from Bn. HQ. Coy. HQ. and each Post, to be at Bde. HQ. FLEURBAIX at 7.45 p.m. 1/4/18.

Battn. HQ. and Coys. will also supply 1 Guide to be at Bde. HQ. FLEURBAIX at 7.45 p.m. to guide transport of incoming unit to Ration Dumps. All Guides will be provided with a chit shewing position of Coys. and No. of Post to be relieved.

(4) <u>MAPS ETC</u>. All Maps of this Area, Documents, Log Books, Trench Stores, will be carefully handed over and receipts obtained. Trenches will be left in a scrupulously clean condition and clean receipts obtained.

(5) <u>Relief Complete</u> will be signalled - "CORN".

(6) <u>Billets</u>. On relief, Companies will move independently to Hutments at ESTAIRES. Route will be:- FLEURBAIX - SAS ST. MAUR - and main ESTAIRES - ARMENTIERES ROAD. Guide will meet Coys. at the Bridge ESTAIRES, G.25.d.95.50. and conduct them to the billets.

Coy. Cdrs. will report in person when their Commands are settled in billets.

(7) <u>MARCH FORMATION</u>. South of the ESTAIRES-ARMENTIERES RAILWAY, Platoons will move at 100 yards distance. North of the Railway, 100 yards distance between Coys. will be maintained.

(8) Administrative Instructions have been issued to all concerned.

A C K N O W L E D G E.

[signature]
Lieut. & A/Adjt.
8th (Irish) Batt. K.L.R.

Issued at 8.30 a.m.
Copies to:-
1. 171 Inf. Bde.
2. 12th Suffolk R.
3. C.O.
4. 2nd in Command.
5. Adjutant.
6. "A" Coy.
7. "B" "
8. "C" "
9. "D" "
10. "H" Coy.
11. Intell. Off. and L.O.
12. M.O.
13. T.O.
14. Q.M.
15. RSM.
16. File.
17. War Diary.
18.

SECRET.   COPY NO...

8th(IRISH) BATT. "THE KING'S" (L'POOL REGIMENT).

Administrative Instructions with
reference to Operation Orders No. 12.
-o-o-o-o-o-o-o-o-o-o-o-o-o-o-o-o-o-o-o-o-o-o-

1/4/18.

(1) All Officers' Kit, Coy. Stores, etc. will be at Coy. Dumps at 8 p.m. ready for removal.

(2) Transport Officer will arrange for the removal of all stores. Lewis Gun Limbers will meet Teams at Coy. Dumps. Field Kitchens will be sent to Hutments ESTAIRES.
Coy. Cdrs. will require their Horses.

(3) The Quartermaster will arrange for hot meals to be provided for the Battalion on arrival at Billets.

(4) Capt. J.H. RILEY will report to Staff Captain at HQ. of 172 Inf. Bde. ESTAIRES at 8.30 a.m. 1/4/18 to take over billets.

(5) Trench Store Lists and Clean certificates will be handed in to Orderly Room by 9 a.m. 2/4/18.

                                                            Lieut. & A/Adjt.
Issued at 8.30 a.m.   8th(Irish) Batt. K.L.R.
TO ALL CONCERNED.

SECRET.   8th(IRISH) BATT. "THE KING'S"(LIVERPOOL REGT).   COPY NO....

OPERATION ORDER NO. 13.

Ref: HAZEBROUCK 5A, 1/100,000.

2/4/18.

(1) This Unit will move to MERVILLE by March Route and from there by No. 12. Train (leaving MERVILLE 2.5 a.m. 3/4/18) on night 2/3rd April 1918.

(2)(a) Order of March will be as follows:-
         HQrs. Company.
         "B" Company.
         "C" "
         "D" "

HQrs. will pass starting point, (location to be notified later) at 10.40 p.m. 2/4/18.
100 yards distance between Companies.
(b) "A" Coy. with Field Kitchen will leave ESTAIRES at 11.45 a.m. on 2/4/18 and report to R.T.O. MERVILLE at 1.30 p.m. 2/4/18. This Company will be the loading Party for 171 Inf. Bde. and will entrain on Train No. 21. which leaves at 11.5 a.m. 3/4/18.

(3) Transport will proceed independently, reporting to R.T.O. MERVILLE, at 11.5 p.m. 2/4/18.

(4) Capt. J.H. RILEY will act as Entraining Officer.
     Entraining will be completed by 1.30 a.m. 3/4/18.

                                               Lieut. & A/Adjt.
                                           8th(Irish) Batt. K.L.R.

Issued at 8 p.m.
Copies to:-
1. 171 Inf. Bde.
2. C.O.
3. 2nd in Commd.
4. Adjutant.
5. Capt. J.H. RILEY.
6. "A" Coy.
7. B "
8. C "
9. D "
10. Sigs. Off.(for HQrs)
11. Intell. Off. & LGO.
12. M.O.
13. T.O.
14. QM.
15. RSM.
16. File.
17. War Diary.
18.

-o-o-o-o-o-o-o-o-

SECRET. 8th(IRISH) BATT."THE KING'S"(L'POOL REGIMENT). COPY NO...

OPERATION ORDER NO. 14.
–o–o–o–o–o–o–o–o–o–o–

Ref: Map LENS 11, 1/100,000. 8/4/18.

(1) This Unit will move to TERRAMESNIL by march route on 8/4/18.

(2) Starting Point will be 4.G.04.06. and movement will be by Coys. at a 100 yards distance in the following order:-
HQrs, A, B, C, and D Coys.
Transport will march 100 yards in rear of Battalion, less Lewis Gun Limbers and Pack animals which will march with Coys. March will commence at 2 p.m.

(3) ROUTE: PAS - THIEVRES - ORVILLE - TERRAMESNIL.

(4) One Officer per Coy. and one N.C.O. from Transport will proceed as Billeting Party. They will parade at Batt. HQ. at 9.45 a.m. 8/4/18.

(5) On arrival at TERRAMESNIL Coy. Cdrs. will immediately select an Alarm Post and notify Battn. HQrs. This must be indicated to all ranks before dismissal.

(6) Batt. HQrs. will close at WARLINCOURT at 2 p.m. 8/4/18, and will open at TERRAMESNIL at that hour.

ACKNOWLEDGE.

Lieut. & A/Adjt.
8th(Irish) Batt. K.L.R.
–o–o–o–o–o–o–o–

Administrative Instructions with reference
to Operation Order No. 14.
–o–o–o–o–o–o–o–o–o–o–o–o–o–o–o–

(1) A motor lorry will report to Q.M.Stores at 11 a.m. 8/4/18. All Officers' Valises, Blankets(rolled in bundles of 10 and labelled), Ordely Room stores will at Q.M.Stores by 12 Noon, 8/4/18.
Transport Officer will arrange to collect HQrs. Mess kit by 1.30 p.m. 8/4/18, and Field Kitchens at that hour also.

(2) DRESS : FULL MARCHING ORDER, leather jerkins will be worn, and greatcoats in packs.

(3) CLEANLINESS: Billets will be left in a scrupulously clean and sanitary condition, and a clean certificate will be obtained from the Billet Warden.

Lieut. & A/Adjt.
8th(Irish) Batt. K.L.R.

Issued at 11 a.m.
Copies as over:-

Copies to:-
1. 171st Inf. Bde.
2. C.O.
3. 2nd in Command.
4. Capt. J.F. JONES M.C.,
5. Adjutant.
6. "A" Coy.
7. "B" "
8. "C" "
9. "D" "
10. O.Qrs."
11. M.O.
12. T.O.
13. Q.M.
14. RSM.
15. File
16. War Diary.

SECRET.   8th (IRISH) BATT. "THE KING'S" (L'POOL R).

OPERATION ORDER NO. 16.

Ref: LENS 11, 1/100,000.   12/4/18.

(1) This Battn. will move by march route via
    AMPLIER - ORVILLE to POMMERA today.

(2) Order of march will be as follows:-
    HQrs, A, B, C, D, and Transport.
    Distance between Coys. and Transport 100 yds.

    Starting Point at S.E.63.25. will be passed
    at 4 p.m.

(3) Battn. HQrs. will close at TERRAMESNIL
    at 3.45 p.m.   It will be at Head of Column
    enroute and will re-open at POMMERA on
    arrival.

(4) Administrative Instructions have been issued
    to all concerned.

    ACKNOWLEDGE.

                                        J B Jones
Issued at 3.45 p.m.   Capt. & Adjt.
Copies to:-   8th (Irish) Batt. K.L.R.
  1. C.O.
  2. 2nd-in-Command.   8. M.G.
  3. "A" Coy.   9. T.O.
  4. "B" "   10. QM.
  5. "C" "   11. RSM.
  6. "D" "   12. File.
  7. HQrs "   13. War Diary.
  7a. Intell. Off.
  7b. Signalling Off.

SECRET.   COPY NO...

8th (IRISH) BATTALION "THE KING'S" (LIVERPOOL REGT).
OPERATION ORDER NO. 17.
-o-o-o-o-o-o-o-o-o-o-

Ref: Sheet 57D, 1/40,000.   14/4/18.

(1) **INFORMATION** (1) In the event of hostile attack the 171 Inf. Bde.
will be responsible for the defence of the H.L. Line
which is on the Right of the IV Corps Front.
The Delimitation of the Brigade Sector will be:-
       Right, O.24.c.Central. - N.22.c.Central.
       Left, I.24.b.2.9. - I.21.a.Central.

(2) **DISPOSITION** (2) Right Front Battalion - 2/6th K.L.R. O.24.c.Central.
   OF BRIGADE   to LOUVENCOURT - ACHEUX RD.
   FOR DEFENCE.   at O.5.b.35.05 inclus-
             The Battn. Hqrs. LEALVILLERS approx. O.15.d.
             Left Front Battalion - 2/7th K.L.R. LOUVENCOURT -
                             ACHEUX ROAD,O.5.b.35.05
                             excl. to I.24.b.2.9.
              Battn. Hqrs. N. of LOUVENCOURT.
             Reserve - 8th K.L.R. - 171 TMB in the Valley E.
                            of VAUCHELLES.
             The forward Battalion will hold the line with 3
             Coys distributed in depth, one Coy. will be held
             in Reserve at Battn. Hqrs.

(3) **DISPOSITION** (3) On arrival at Assembly Position Coys. will deploy
   OF THE BATTN. in Platoon Artillery Formations - Front Coys. to
              be as near the Crest as possible.
             Order of Battle:-
                Right Front Coy.   "A" Coy.
                Left   "   "   "B" "
                Right Rear "   "C" "
                Left   "   "   "D" "

(4) **MACHINE GUNS** (4) Machine Guns will be disposed roughly as under:-

"A" Coy.
{ 2 Guns O.10.a.70.90.)
{ 2 " O.13.a.30.60.) Covering LEALVILLERS
{   ) approaches.
{ 2 " O.17.b.40.60.) Covering Road Rly. and exits
{ 2 " O.11.d.60.30.) from ACHEUX.
{ 2 " O.5.d.30.20.) Covering Valley running O.6.
{ 2 " O.5.b.30.90.) c.b. and approaches to
{   ) LOUVENCOURT.

"A" Coy. & Hq. { 4 " Res. O.16.a.20.60.

"B" Coy.
{ 2 " I.29.d.40.20. Covering approaches LOUVENCOURT.
{ 2 " I.29.d.10.90.
{ 4 " I.18.a.   "   " HQS - MES
{   - ACHEM.
{ 4 " J.13.a.   " Plateau S. of MES-LEN-
{   ARTOIS.

"B" Coy. Hq. { 4 " by ACHEUX - LOUVENCOURT, I.22.b.

(5) **MEDICAL.** (5) AID POST will be established at Battn. Hq.

(6) **BATTN. HQ** (6) Approx. O.3.a.60.90.

(7) **REPORTS** (7) To Battn. Hqrs.

ACKNOWLEDGE.

                                                        Capt. & Adjt.
                                                        8th (Irish) Battn. K.L.R.

Issued at 10.30 p.m.
To:- 1. 171 Inf. Bde.   8. Adjt.
    2. 2/6th K.L.R.   9. "A" Coy.
    3. 2/7th K.L.R.   10. "B" "   16. T.O.
    4. 171 LTMB   11. "C" "   17. QM
    5. 37th M.G. Battn. 12. "D" "   18. M.O.
    6. C.O.   13. Hqrs.   19. RSM
    7. 2nd in Cmd.   14. Sign. Off. 20. File
                          15. Intell. Off. 21. War Diary

SECRET.

8th (IRISH) BATTALION "THE KING'S" (L'POOL REGIMENT).
OPERATION ORDER NO. 17.
-:o:-:o:-:o:-:o:-:o:-:o:-:o:-:o:-:o:-

COPY No. 21

Ref: Sheet 57D, 1/40,000.   14/4/18.

(1) **INFORMATION** (1)- In the event of heavy hostile attack the 171
Inf. Bde. will be responsible for the defence of the
RED Line which is on the Right of the IV Corps Front.
The delimitations of the Bde. Sector will be:-
Right: O.24.c.Central. - B.22.c.Central.
Left : I.24.b.2.9. - I.21.a.Central.

(2) **DISPOSITION** (2) Right Front Batt: 2/6th K.L.R. O.24.c.Central
OF BRIGADE   to LOUVENCOURT - ACHEUX ROAD at O.5.b.85.05. incl.
FOR DEFENCE.   Battn. Hqrs. LEALVILLERS approx. O.15.d.
Left Front Batt : 2/7th K.L.R. LOUVENCOURT -
ACHEUX Rd. O.5.b.85.05. exclus. to I.24.b.2.9.
Battn. Hq. N. of LOUVENCOURT.
Reserve: 8th K.L.R. and 171 LTMB in the valley
S. of VAUCHELLES.
The Forward Battalion will hold the line with 3 Companies
distributed in depth. One coy. will be held in reserve
at Battn. Hqrs.

(3) **DISPOSITION** (3) On arrival at assembly position, Coys. will deploy
OF THE BATTN.   in platoon artillery formation - front coys. to be as
near the Crest as possible.
Order of Battle.
Right Front Coy.   "A" Coy.
Left   "   "   "B" "
Right Rear "   "C" "
Left   "   "   "D" "

(4) **MACHINE GUNS** (4)- Machine Guns will be disposed roughly as under:-
(2 Guns O.20.a.70.90.) covering LEALVILLERS approaches.
(2 "   O.18.a.50.60.)   do.
(2 "   O.17.b.40.80.)
"A" Coy (2 "   O.11.d.80.80.) " ROAD METY. and exits from
(2 "   O.5.d.20.20.)   ACHEUX
(2 "   O.5.b.80.90.) " Valley running O.6.c.b. and
                          approaches to LOUVENCOURT.
"A" Coy. & HQ 4 "   Reserve. O.18.a.20.60.
(2 "   I.29.c.40.80.   covering approaches LOUVENCOURT.
"B" Coy (2 "   I.29.d.10.90.
(4 "   I.13.a.   ) covering approaches BUS-LES-ARTOIS.
(4 "   J.12.a.   " plateau N. of BUS-LES-ARTOIS.
"B" Coy. & HQ 4 "   by AUTHIE - LOUVENCOURT, I.22.b.

(5) **MEDICAL** (5) Aid Post will be established at Battn. HQ.

(6) **BATTN. HQ** (6) Approx. O.3.a.60.00.

(7) **REPORTS** (7) to Battn. HQ.

ACKNOWLEDGE.

                                         J.B.Jones
                                         Capt. & Adjt.
                                         8th (Irish) Batt. K.L.R.
Issued at 10.20 p.m.
To:- 1. 171 Inf. Bde.   9. "A" Coy.
     2. 2/6th K.L.R.   10. "B" "
     3. 2/7th   "   11. "C" "
     4. 171 LTMB   12. "D" "   17. JM.
     5. 57 MG. Bn.   13. Hqrs. "   18. MO.
     6. C.O.   14. Sigs. Off.   19. RSM.
     7. 2nd in Cd.   15. Intell. Off.   20. File.
     8. Adjt.   16. T.O.   21. War Diary.

SECRET.   COPY NO. 16

8th (IRISH) BATTALION "THE KING'S" (L'POOL REGIMENT).
GENERAL INSTRUCTIONS ISSUED WITH REFERENCE
TO OPERATION ORDER NO. 17, dated 14/4/18.
-o-o-o-o-o-o-o-o-o-o-o-o-o-o-o-o-o-o-o-o-o-o-o-o-o-o-

14/4/18.

(1) In the event of this scheme being put into operation
the following instructions will become operative:-

(a) DRESS & EQUIPMENT. Fighting order. Coys. will at
once draw from Limbers, SAA, to equip to 170 rounds per
man, bombs, Ground Flares, and S.O.S. Flares.
Rifle Bombs will be detonated immediately after arrival
at assembly position. The Asst. Adjt. will supervise
the issue. Coys. will have carrying parties permanently
detailed for this work from "B" Team.

(b) RATIONS & WATER. Unexpended portion of day's ration and
Iron Ration will be carried. Waterbottles will be
filled. The Quartermaster will organise hot food
supplied immediately Battalion moves into position.

(c) SURPLUS STORES. All Blankets, Packs, Mess Kits, and
other surplus stores will be dumped in Company Lines and
left under the charge of Senior Coy. N.C.O. on "B" Team.

(d) "B" TEAM. Will immediately come under command of Major
F.H. DOWNING and will be responsible for collecting surplus
kit and striking camp if necessary.

(2) ORDER OF MARCH AND PROBABLE ROUTE NUMBERS:-
March to Assembly Position will be in the order
Hqrs, A, B, C, and D Companies.
Movement from present location will be via Northern Exit
- Bde. Hqrs. and via VAUCHELLES, in rear of 2/6th K.L.R.

(3) TRANSPORT. 1st Line Transport, less L.G. Limbers and Pack
Mules which will follow Companies, and such vehicles as
may be detailed later, will proceed to position of assembly
as early as possible after the Battalion.
Precedence of Route will be in the following order:-
57th Bn.M.G.C., - 2/6th K.L.R. - 2/7th K.L.R. -
8th K.L.R. - 2/2nd Wessex Field Amb.

Issued at 11.30 p.m.
To:-
1. C.O.
2. 2nd in CC.   Capt. & Adjt.
3. Adjt.   11. M.O.   8th (Irish) Batt. K.L.R.
4. "A" Coy.   12. QM.
5. "B" "   13. TO.
6. "C" "   14. RSM.
7. "D" "   15. File.
8. Hqrs "   16. War Diary.
9. Sigs. Of.
10. Intell. Off.

SECRET.   COPY NO. 14.

8th (IRISH) BATTALION "THE KING'S" (L'POOL REGT).
GENERAL INSTRUCTIONS WITH REFERENCE TO
OPERATION ORDER NO. 18.

15/4/18.

1. All orders contained in Para. 1. of General Instrns. issued with O.O. 17. of 14/4/18 will be adhered to.

2. March to assembly positions will be in the order Hqrs., B, A, C, and D Coys. Movement from present location will be via Northern Exit and will probably be in rear of 2/6th KLR.

3. 1st Line Transport, (less L.G. Limbers and Pack Mules which will follow Coys), and such vehicles as may be detailed later, will proceed to Assembly area as early as possible after the Battalion. Precedence of route will be in the following order:- 57th M.G. Bttn., 2/7th KLR, 2/6th MBR, 8th KLR, 171 LTMB, and 2/2nd Wessex Field Ambulance.

J.F. Joze
Capt. & Adjt.
8th (Irish) Batt. K. L. R.

Issued at 7 p.m.

TO ALL RECIPIENTS OF OPERATION ORDER NO. 18.

SECRET.   COPY No. 19
            8th (IRISH) BATTALION "THE KING'S" (L'POOL REGIMENT).
                        OPERATION ORDER NO. 13.
            ....

Ref: Sheet 57D, 1/40,000.   18/4/18.

    (1) INFORMATION(1):- In the event of a heavy hostile attack the
                171st Inf. Bde. may be called upon for the defence of that
                portion of the RED Line which is on the Left of the IV
                Corps Front. Delimitations of the Bde. sector will be:-

                    Right : I.18.d.0. - J.21.a.Central.
                    Left : D.28.Central - C.29.Central.

    (2) DISPOSITION OF BRIGADE FOR DEFENCE(2): Right Front Battn -
                2/6th K.L.R. - I.18.d.0.0. to J.15.b.3.3.
                Battn. HQ. in J.7.a.
                Left Front Battn : 2/7th K.L.R. J.15.b.3.3. - D.28.Central.
                Battn. HQ. in neighbourhood of COIGNEUX.
                Reserve Battn : 8th L'Pool Irish : J.8.a & b.
                Battn. HQ. in J.8.a.
                171 LTMB. about J.1.a.Central.
                Battalions will adopt artillery formations on arrival
                at assembly positions as they may required for counter
                attack instead of manning the RED Line.   If the RED Line
                is manned Battalions will hold it with 3 Coys. distributed
                in depth, and one Coy. in Reserve at Battn. HQ.

    (3) DISPOSITION OF THE BATTALION(3):- On arrival at Assembly position
                Companies will deploy in platoon Artillery Formation -
                facing E. Order of Battle:-
                    Right Front Coy. "A" Coy.
                    Left   "   " "B" "
                    Right Rear "   "C" "
                    Left   "   "   "D" "

    (4) MACHINE GUNS(4):- Machine Guns will be disposed roughly as
                under:-
                     (2 Guns J.14.b.75.20.   covering roads.
        "C" Coy.   (2 "   J.15.a.50.10.   "   valley to SAILLY AU BOIS.
                     (2 "   J.9.a.40.60.   "   road and valley approach to
                                                      COIGNEUX.

                     (2 "   J.3.d.0.60.   approaches from BAYENCOURT.
                     (2 "   D.28.b.30.10. covering valley through 29 and 30.
        "C" Coy.   (2 "   I.23.a.50.10.   "   approaches to BOUZINE.
        & HQ.   (4 "   D.27.a.

    (5) LIAISON(5): Liaison with forward Battalions will be maintained
                by means of Patrols which will be sent out at 15 minute
                intervals.   "A" Coy. will maintain touch with 2/6th KLR.
                "B" Coy. will maintain touch with 2/7th K.L.R.   All
                information will be passed speedily to Battn. HQ.

    (6) MEDICAL (6): Aid Post will be established adjacent to Battn. HQ.

    (7) BATTN.HQRS(7): About J.8.a.Central.

    (8) REPORTS (8)   To Battn. Hqrs.

    ACKNOWLEDGE.
                                                    J.F. Hale
                                                  Capt. & Adjt.
    Issued at 6 p.m.   8th (Irish) Batt. K.L.R.
    To:-
        1. 171 Inf. Bde.
        2. 2/6th KLR.   11. Hqrs. Coy.
        3. 2/7th KLR.   12. Sig. Off.
        4. 171 LTMB.   13. Intell. Off.
        5. C.O.   14. MO.
        6. 2nd i/c   15. TO.
        7. "A" Coy.   16. QM.
        8. "B" "   17. RSM.
        9. "C" "   18. File.
       10. "D" "   19. War Diary.
                                20.
                        -o-o-o-o-o-o-

SECRET.   COPY NO..
           8th(IRISH) BATTALION "THE KING'S(L'POOL R).
                  OPERATION ORDER NO.19.
              -o-o-o-o-o-o-o-o-o-o-o-o-
Ref: Sheet 57 D, 1/40,000.   16/4/18.
                                                                today.

(1) This Battalion will move by march route/via S.
    Exit of wood - Bde.HQ. - Crossroads I.16.a.90.45. -
    THIEVRES - FANKCRON to Camp S. of PAS.

(2) Order of march will be HQrs, A, B, C, and D Coys.
    Starting Point at Bde.HQ. will be passed at 10.37
    a.m.   100 yards distance will be maintained between
    Coys. on the march.

(3) Transport will be Brigaded and will follow 171 Bde.HQ. &   171
    LTMB and 2/7th K.L.R.   Head of transport column   /
    passes cross roads AUTHIE at 11.13 a.m.   100 yards
    distance will be maintained between Unit's transport
    on the march.

(4) One Officer from each Coy.(on cycles) and one NCO.
    mounted for Transport and QM.Stores will report as advance
    party to Staff Captain at the Church, PAS, at 11 a.m.

(5) Battn.HQ. will close at AUTHIE at 10.15 a.m.
    It will be at head of column en route and will reopen
    immediately upon arrival at PAS.

       ACKNOWLEDGE.
                                                    [signature]
Issued at 7.30 a.m.   Capt. & Adjt.
To: 1. 171 Inf. Bde.   8th(Irish) Batt. K.L.R.
    2. C.O.   10. Sigs.Off.
    3. 2nd i/c.   11. Intell.Off.
    4. Adjt.   12. M.O.
    5. "A" Coy.   13. T.O.
    6. "B" "   14. QM.
    7. "C" "   15. R.S.M.
    8. "D" "   16. File.
    9. HQrs "   17. War Diary.
              -o-o-o-o-o-o-o-o-o-o-o-o-

SECRET.   COPY NO..
           8th(IRISH) BATTALION "THE KING'S"(L'POOL R).
           Administrative Instructions with reference
                  to Operation Order 19.
              -o-o-o-o-o-o-o-o-o-o-o-o-o-o-o-o-o-
                                                     16/4/18.

(1) All Officers' Valises, Mess Kit, Blankets(neatly rolled
    in bundles of 10 and labelled) and other stores will be
    dumped at QM.Stores at 9 a.m.
(2) QM. will return all extra blankets(in 10s) issued to
    the Unit to the crucifix in SE. corner of wood.
(3) Dress will be Marching Order.   Jerkins will be carried
    on top of packs under oil sheets.
(4) QM. will detail a Guide for motor lorry to report to
    Bde.HQ. at 8.45 a.m.   Lorry will do one journey only.
(5) Tents will not be struck.

                                                    [signature]
                                                    Capt. & Adjt.
Issued to all recipients of   8th(Irish) Batt. K.L.R.
Operation Order No.19.(except 171 Bde)
At 7.30 a.m.
              -o-o-o-o-o-o-o-o-o-o-o-

TO ALL RECIPIENTS OF O.O. NO. 20.

SCRT.   O.O. No. 18 is cancelled, and O.O. NO. 20.
substituted. The Adminstrativ Instructions issued on
19/4/18 with reference to O.O. NO. 18 will apply to O.O. NO. 20.

21/4/18.

Capt. & Adjt
8th (Irish) Batt. KLR.

TO ALL RECIPIENTS OF GENERAL INSTRUCTIONS WITH REFERENCE TO
OPERATION ORDERS NOS. 18 and 20.

The following amendments will be made to General Instructions issued with reference to O.Os. 18 and 20. **Para. 5. TRANSPORT.** will be amended to read - "Four limbers only will accompany the Unit". (these will be loaded in accordance with scale which has been issued to all concerned). "The remainder of the transport will be Brigaded under the Staff Captain and will remain at the present Transport Lines" **Para. 6. DUMPS.** - line 5. J.3.d.4.6. should read J.3.b.5.7. The Battn. and Coy. Dumps will consist of 5 boxes S.A.A. each. **Para. 8. PRISONERS OF WAR.** The following addition will be made :- The N.C.O. i/c escort must be in possession of a note giving the locality and time of capture. Other ranks will only be examined for arms before arrival at Div'l Cage, but Officers will be searched immediately and all maps, documents, etc. placed in a sandbag and handed to the N.C.O. i/c escort. These will be handed to the Divl. I.O. and a receipt obtained for same.

[signature]
Capt. & Adjt.
8th (Irish) Batt. K.L.R.

23/4/18.

Ref: 57D, NE.

8th (IRISH) BATT. "THE KING'S" (L'POOL R).
APPENDIX "A" TO O.O. 20.

COMMUNICATIONS. B'tween Battalions, and Bde. HQ. and other Units.

(1)(a) A Visual Station will be established before the arrival of the Battalion at the Assembly area at approx. J.8.a.40.50. and will be in communication with the following Visual Stations:-

    Bde. HQ.   approx. I.11.b.60.05.
    2/6th KLR.   "   J.7.b.70.10.
    2/7th KLR.   "   J.3.c.70.05.

(b) Messages from Bde. F.C.P. to 2/7th KLR. will be transmitted through 8th KLR. Visual Station.

(c) If enemy attacks RED LINE, DD Messages will be sent to the Bde. Forward Command Post.

(d) All communication with Bde. F.C.P. will be carried on by means of Visual and Runners, until telephonic communication is established by Bde. Signal Section.

( ) Adv. Bde. HQ. will be at J.2.b.3.8.

B'tween Battn. HQ. and Company HQ.

In Assembly Positions and in advance communication will be maintained by Visual and Runner.

(b) If the Battalion is required to garrison any portion of the RED LINE or other defensive system communication will be maintained by Visual and Runner until telephonic communication has been installed. This will be done under Battn. HQ. arrangements, immediately definite positions are taken up.

All messages must be sent by at least two methods (i.e. Visual and Runner, or Telephone and Runner). Runners will carry messages in Right Top Pocket of Tunic. Nothing else will be carried in this pocket.

                                                          Capt. & Adjt,
                                                          8th (Irish) Bn. K. L. R.

23/4/18.

8th (IRISH) BATT. "THE KING'S" (L'POOL REGT).

SECRET.

AMENDMENT AND ADDENDUM TO OPERATION ORDER NO. 20.

(1)(a) A French Battalion will now hold the portion of the Brigade Front from J.14. Central to J.9.b.20.30.

(b) 2/6th K.L.R. will remain in their assembly formations and await further orders in the event of the Brigade being ordered to hold the RED LINE.

(2) The 577 Army Troops Coy. R.E. located at COIGNEUX - SOUASTRE VALLEY D.27.d.Central is now placed at the disposal of B.G.C. 171 Inf. Bde. in the event of an attack. The Coy. will assemble in ST. LEGER and will be held in Brigade Reserve.

ACKNOWLEDGE.

23/4/18.

Capt. & Adjt.
8th (Irish) Batt. K.L.R.

-o-o-o-o-o-o-

SECRET.   COPY No. 19
                 8th(IRISH) BATT. "THE KING'S"(L'POOL REGIMENT).
                            OPERATION ORDER NO. 20.

Ref: Sheet 57D. 1/40,000.   20/4/18.

(1) **INFORMATION** (1) There are indications that an enemy attack
                        may be launched on this front at an early date. In
                        this event, the 171 Inf. Bd. will move forward and occupy
                        positions of assembly behind the RED LINE from
                        J.14.Central to the Road at J.28.c.0.0. inclus-

(2) **DISPOSITION OF THE BRIGADE IN ASSEMBLY POSITIONS AND**
    PROBABLE ACTION:
               Right Battn. 2/6th K.L.R.   Bn.HQ. J.7.a.70.10.
               Left   "   2/7th K.L.R.   "   J.3.c.70.05.
               Reserve "   8th K.L.R.   "   J.9.a. 171 LYNDE.
               Bde.HQ.   I.11.b.60.05.

         Boundaries between Bde. on Right and Left and between
    Units will be as follows:-
         Southern Boundary, Between 2/6th K.L.R. and 63rd Inf.
                             Bd. J.14.Central to I.12.c.0.5.
         Centre Boundary :   Between 2/6th K.L.R. and 2/7th K.L.R.
                             The road at J.9.b.20.20.(inclus.to Right Bn) to
                             J.1.d.95.05.
         Northern Boundary: Between 2/7th K.L.R. and 172nd Inf.
                             Bd. J.28.c.0.0. to J.25.Central.

         The Brigade may be required either to :-
    (a) Move forward and counter-attack in the Centre Divl.
         Sector K.21.c. to L.7.b.

    (b) Move forward and counter attack in the Left Divl.
         Sector L.7.b. to F.25.a., or

    (c) To hold the RED LINE.

                In the event of (a) & (b) the probable jumping off
    place for counter attack Battalions will be CHATEAU DE LA
    HAIE SWITCH.
                In the event of (c) Battalions in the line will hold
    the line with 2 or 3 Companies distributed in depth. The
    remaining Coy. or Coys. will be in reserve near Battalion
    Headquarters.

(3) **DISPOSITIONS OF THE BATTALION** (3) On arrival at Assembly
              positions - J.9.a. and B, Companies will deploy in
              Platoon Artillery formation facing East. Order of battle
              will be :-   Right Front Coy.   "A" Coy.
                            Left   "   "   "B" "
                            Right Rear "   "C" "
                            Left   "   "   "D" "
                            Battalion Hqrs.   J.9.a.

(4) **MACHINE GUNS** (4) Machine Guns will be disposed roughly as
         under:-
             (2 Guns J.14.b.70.20.   covering roads.
    "C" Coy. (2 "   J.15.a.30.30.   " valley to BAILLY AU BOIS.
             (2 "   J.9.a.40.60.   " road and valley approach to
                                              COIGNEUX.

             (2 "   J.3.d.00.50.   approaches from BETHENCOURT.
             (2 "   L.28.b.30.10.   covering valley through 29 and 30.
             (2 "   I.23.a.60.10.   "   approaches to SOUASTRE.
    "C" Coy. (
    & HQ.   (4 "   J.27.a.

- 2 -

(5) **COMMUNICATIONS**(5): As per appendix "A".

(6) **CARRYING PLATOONS**(6) Two Platoons of "D" Coy. will report to Battn. HQ. Immediately upon arrival at Assembly area. They will be employed for the purpose of carrying S.A.A. and material, and formation of dumps.

(7) **LIAISON**(7) Liaison with forward and flank troops will be maintained by means of patrols which will be sent out at 30 minute intervals. "A" Coy. will maintain touch with 2/6th K.L.R. and Battn of 63rd Bde. on Right. "B" Coy. will maintain touch with 2/7th K.L.R. and Battn. of 172 Inf. Bde. on Left. Patrols will also establish lateral liaison from Battn.HQ. All information will be passed speedily to Battn.HQ.

(8) **STRAGGLERS' POSTS**(8) will be formed at Fork Roads at J.9.b.30.75. and J.1.c.60.00. Stragglers will be sent back to Battn.HQ. under escort.

(9) **MEDICAL**(9)(a) Regtl. Aid Post will be formed in vicinity of Battn. HQ. Evacuations to Collecting Post(2/2nd Wessex Field Amb) at I.12.a.1.3. will be by Hand Carriers and Wheeled Stretcher Carriers to be detailed by 2/2nd Wessex Field Ambulance.
(b) A Guide will be sent to Collecting Post at I.12.a.1.3. to indicate location of Regtl. Aid Post.

(10) **REPORTS**(10) To Battalion HQrs.

Administrative Instructions and orders for march to assembly position have been issued to all concerned.

A C K N O W L E D G E.

Capt. & Adjt.
8 th(Irish) Battn. K.L.R.

Issued at 9.30 p.m.
Copies to:-
1. 171 Inf. Bde.
2. 2/6th K.L.R.
3. 2/7th K.L.R.
4. C.O.
5. 2nd i/c.
6. Adjt.
7. Intell.Off.
8. Sigs.Off.
9. "A" Coy.
10. "B" "
11. "C" "
12. "D" "
13. HQ "
14. T.O.
15. Q.M.
16. M.O.
17. RSM.
18. File.
19. War Diary.
20.

-o-o-o-o-o-o-o-o-

8th (Irish) Bat'n The King's Liverpool Regiment WAR DIARY
INTELLIGENCE SUMMARY
MAY 1918

Army Form C. 2118.

Place	Date	Hour	Summary of Events and Information	Remarks and references to Appendices
PAS 57 D '/20000 C.27.E.	1st May		Strength 37 Officers 960 Other Ranks. Batt'n at work in Pod Line East of SOUASTRE	
	2nd May		Training - Musketry, Arms Drill, Lewis Gun, Reconnaissance of forward Area by Coy Commanders	
	3rd&4th		Training - Practice Attack over ground in C.27 & C.28.	
	5th May		Training - (Musketry, Arms Drill, Lewis Gun)	
	6th May		Move to Forward Area and Relieved 1/5 Lancs Fusiliers in Support to the Left Brigade Sector of Auricourt Front. Batt. H.Q. Ref 57 DNE 1/20000 E.29 a. 3.70. Order of Battle Right "B" Coy. Centre "A" Coy. Left "C" Coy. Reserve "D" Coy. Work on forward trenches and own Sector - Musketry & Rifle Grenade Practice. Casualties OR. 3 killed 32 wounded.	(1)
GONNECOURT E.29	15th May		Relieved in Line by 2/4th Royal N. Lancs Regt. and went to positions in The Chateau de-la-Haie Switch Batt. H.Q. Ref 57 DNE. T.6.6. Working Parties to forward area Casualties 2 OR. wounded (Relieved 10th. K.L.R.)	(2)
	13 May		Major T.H. Bowring took over Command of "B" Coy. Capt. R. Jones relinquished the appointment of Adjutant and assumed duties	

E. O'Neill
Lieut. Col. Commanding 8th (Irish) Bat'n King's Liverpool

8th (Irish) Batt. "The King's"
Liverpool Regiment

Army Form C. 2118.

WAR DIARY
INTELLIGENCE SUMMARY.
(Erase heading not required.)

MAY 1918.

Place	Date	Hour	Summary of Events and Information	Remarks and references to Appendices
Chateau de la Haie 57D.N.E.76			2nd in Command of the Battalion - Appointed acting Major.	
			Relieved by 27th K.R.R. moving to their billets in COIGNEUX - B.H.Q. I.9.a.70.40.	(3)
COIGNEUX I.9.a.	17th May		Working parties to forward area. Reconnaissance of new sector by Officers & N.C.O.s	
	18-20 May		Cleaning up. Inspection parades. musketry. Working parties.	
	21st May		Moved forward and Relieved 9th K.R.R. in front line - Left Batt. Sector of Right Brigade of the Divisional Front. B.H.Q. E.28.a.40.10. Order of Battle. Front. "D" Coy. Support "C" Coy. Reserve "B" Coy. Headquarters "A" Coy.	(4)
GOMMECOURT			Vigorous patrolling of N.M.L. Enemy Patrols carried out during the whole tour. Enemy distributed heavy artillery fire at intervals over sector. Daylight fighting patrols with slight artillery bombardment carried out as follows:-	
	27th May		by "D" Coy (2/Lt Snowdge) no Identification	(5)
	29th May		by D.Coy & A.Coy (2/Lt Harrison) no Identification	(6)
			Inter Coy Reliefs D by A on 25th May. A by B on 28th May.	
			Casualties to 31st May - Killed 1 Off. 5 O.R. Wounded 1 Off. 13 O.R.	
	18th May		Major 9th Browning reported for duty with the 172 Inf. Bde.	
	31st May		Strength 26 Officers 680 O.R.s	

E. O. J. O.K.
Lieut Col. Commanding 8th (Irish) Batt King's Liverpool Regt.

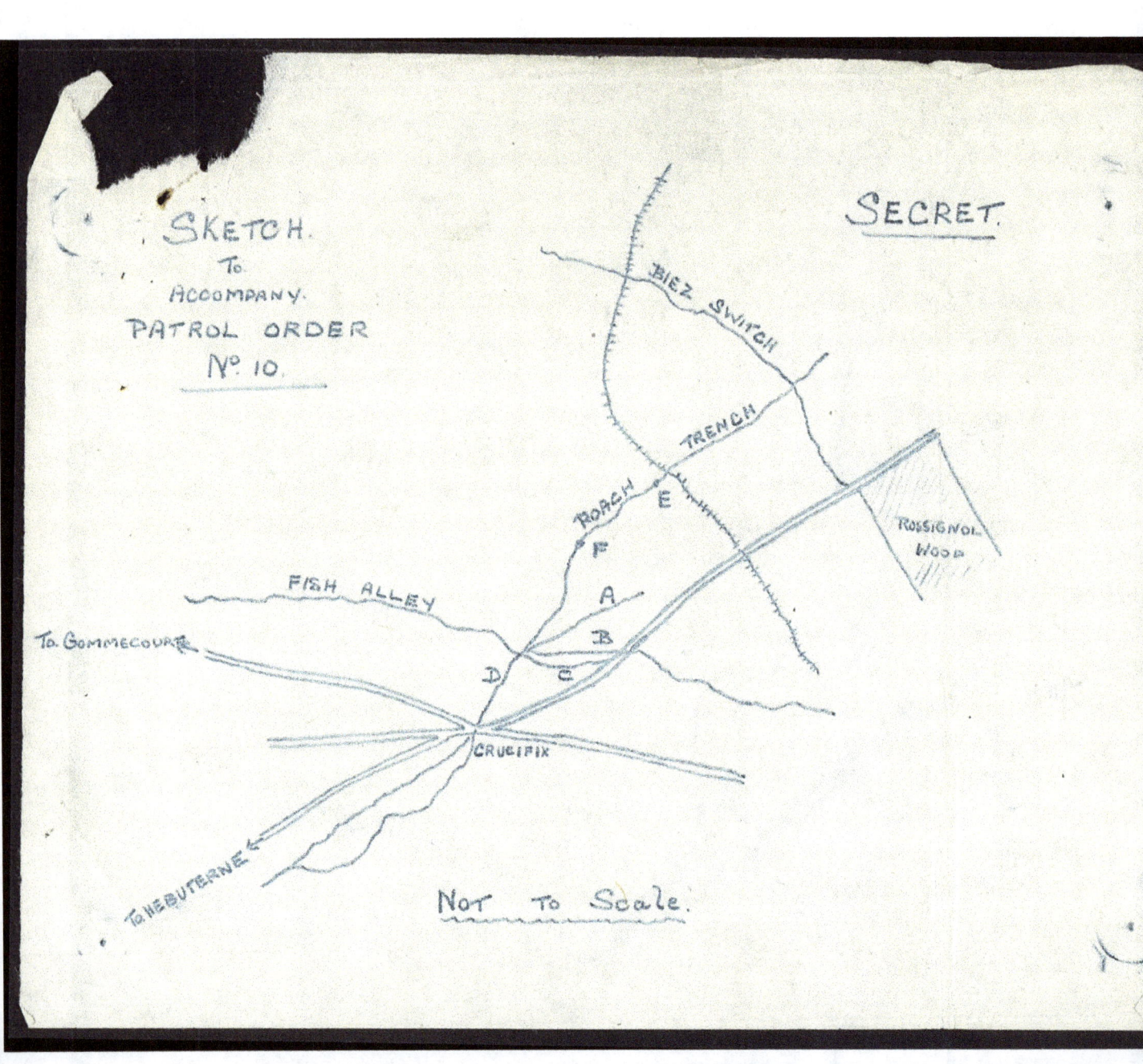

War Diary.

A.R.
57th Division.

Herewith original War Diary
for 8th (Irish) Bn K.L.R. for the month
of June 1918.

W. Hornley 2/Lt
for Major
1/7/18.   Commdg 8th (Irish) Bn K.L.R.

8TH (IRISH) BN.,
"THE KING'S"
(LIVERPOOL REGT)
No. 2503

SECRET.   COPY NO. 5
            8th (IRISH) BATTALION "THE KING'S" (L'POOL R).
                       OPERATION ORDER NO. 23.
            =O=O=O=O=O=O=O=O=O=O=O=O=O=O=O=O=O=O=O=

Ref: Map 57D, 1/40,000.   5/5/18.

(1) This Battalion will relieve the 1/5th Bn. Lan. Fus. in Support
    to the Left Sector of the Centre Divisional Front on the
    night 6/7th May 1918.

(2)(a) Battalion will move from present location in the order
       HQr, C, A, B, and D Coy. at 3.15 p.m. passing Bde. Starting
       Point, C.17.c.50.10. at 3.30 p.m.   Companies will
       move at 100 yards distance WEST of SOUASTRE, and by platoons
       at 200 yards distance EAST of SOUASTRE.
    (b) The Battalion will halt immediately East of SOUASTRE for
        tea and will move forward at 8.45 p.m.
    (c) Guides will await arrival of Unit at Junction of
        MONQUEVILLER - GOMMECOURT ROAD with old enemy front line
        at E.28.c.60.30. at 10.15 p.m.

(3) Order of Battle on taking over Sector will be as follows:-
        Right Front Coy: "B" Coy. HQr. E.29.a.17.26.
        Centre   "   "   "A" "   "   E.29.a.70.32.
        Left   "   "   "C" "   "   E.29.b.35.60.
        Reserve Company: "D" "   "   E.29.a.25.95.
        Battn. HQrs. at E.29.a.35.72.
    O.C. Companies will take over exact dispositions of similar
    lettered Companies of 1/5th Bn. Lan. Fus.

(4)(a) One Officer and 4 N.C.Os. per Coy. and one Officer and
       2 N.C.Os. for Battn. HQ. will proceed to the line to-morrow
       at 9 a.m. for the purpose of taking over.
    (b) All Maps, Defence Schemes, Plans of Defence Schemes will
        be taken over.
    (c) Scheme for manning the RED LINE and counter attacking
        BEER TRENCH will be handed over to Unit taking over this Camp.

(5) Transport Lines, QM. Stores, and Rear HQr. will be taken
    over at COUIN, J.7.a.   Advance Party will proceed to take
    over at 9 a.m. to-morrow.

(6) Relief Complete will be reported by wire, using Code Word
    "SAP".

(7) Battn. HQ. will close at present location at 3 p.m. 6/5/18.
    Rear HQ. will re-open at COUIN at that time. Forward HQ.
    - head of column en route - opening at E.29.a.35.72. at
    10.15 p.m. 6/5/18.

    Administrative Instruction have been issued to all concerned.

    ACKNOWLEDGE.

                                            J.F. Jones
                                            Capt. & Adjt.
Issued at 10.30 p.m.   8th (Irish) att. K.L.R.
Copies to:-
    1. 171 Inf. Bde,   12. M.O.
    2. 1/5th Lan. Fus.   13. QM.
    3. C.O.   14. TO.
    4. 2nd i/c   15. RSM.
    5. Adjt.   16. War Diary.
    6. Intell. Off.   17. File.
    7. Sig. Off.
    8. HQ Coy.
    9 - 12. A, B, C, D, Coy.

            =O=O=O=O=O=O=O=

8th (Irish) BATT. "THE KING'S" (L
OPERATION ORDER NO. 24.

REF. 57B.NE.1/20,000.   14/5/18.

(1)(a) This Battalion will be relieved in Support
    positions – left Brigade Sub-Sector – on night
    14/15th May, 1918, by 2/4th L.N.Lan.R.
    (b) On relief the Battalion will move to LA HAIE
    SWITCH, relieving 2/6th K.L.R.

(2) One guide per Battle Position and one Guide for
    Battn. and Company HQrs. will meet incoming Unit at
    Junction of old German Front Line and FONQUEVILLERS
    – GOMMECOURT ROAD (approx. N.28.c.7.4.) at 3.45 pm.
    14/5/18.   They will lead reliefs to Battle
    Positions and from thence to living quarters.

(3) On relief Companies will move off independently
    to LA HAIE SWITCH, relieving same letters of
    2/6th K.L.R.   Movement will be by platoons
    at 200 yards distance.   All roads and tracks
    will be reconnoitred by daylight 14/5/18.

(4)(a) Defence Schemes, Trench Stores and particulars
    of working parties and work in progress and proposed
    will be carefully handed over to incoming Unit –
    receipts being obtained.
    (b) Capt. A.A.GARBERRY., MC., and one N.C.O. for HQrs.
    and one Officer and one N.C.O. per Company will
    proceed to LA HAIE SWITCH at 4 p.m. 14/5/18 for
    the purpose of taking over.

(5) Completion of relief will be reported by the Code
    word "DO".

(6) Battn.HQ. will close at present location at
    11 p.m. 14/5/18 and will open at LA HAIE SWITCH
    at that hour.

    Administrative Instructions have been issued to
    all concerned.

    ACKNOWLEDGE.   Capt. & Adjt.
                                     8 (8th (Irish) Bn.K.L.R.

(ocer)

Copies to:-

   1. 170th Inf.Bde.
   2. 171st Inf.Bde.
   3. 2/4th L.N.Lan.R.
   4. C.O.
   5. HQrs.Officers.
  6 - 9. 4 Companies.
 10. T.O.and Q.M.
 11. File.
 12. War Diary.

Secret   8th (Irish) Bn K.L.R.   Copy No.
                         50 25   3.
Ref. 57.D.R9. 1/20,000

1(a) This Bn. will be relieved in
LA HAIE SWITCH on night of 17/18
May 1918, by 2/7th K.L.R.
(b) On relief the Bn. will move to
billets vacated by 2/7th K.L.R. at COIGNEUX.

2(a) Advance parties of one
Officer and one NCO for HQ
and one Officer and one NCO
per Company will proceed to COIGNEUX
at 2 p.m. 17.5.18
(b) Intelligence Officer will take 2 Runners
for Bn. HQ. and 2 Runners per
Company to COIGNEUX at 2 p.m.
17.5.18. These will return
to present locations and guide
Companies on relief.

(3) All defence schemes, maps and
trench stores will be carefully
handed over and receipts taken.
Advance parties will take over
all defence schemes, maps and
trench stores at new locations.

(4) Companies will move off independently on relief – 200 yds. distance being maintained between platoons.

(5) Completion of relief will be reported by code word DAPHNE.

(6) Bn HQ will close at CHATEAU DE LA HAIE at 8pm and will open at COIGNEUX at that time.

Administrative Instructions have been issued to all concerned.

Acknowledge.

C. Stansberry
Capt.
Capt Adjt
7th KRR

Copies to:-
1. 171 Inf Bde
2. 2/7th KRR
3. CO
4. HQ Coy
5-9. 5 Coys
10. TO QM
11. MO
12. War Diary

SECRET.   COPY NO....16
        8th (IRISH) BATTALION "THE KING'S (L'POOL R).
                    OPERATION ORDER NO. 26.

Ref: 57 D., NE., 1/20,000.   20.5.18.

   (1) This Battalion will relieve the 9th Bn. K.L.R. Left
       Battn. Right Sub-sector on the night 21/22 May 1918.

   (2)(a) Battn. will move from present location in the order
       HQ., "D", "C", "B", and "A" Coys. at 7.30 p.m. Platoons
       will move at 200 yards distance, to move via Road Junctions
       J.4.c.60.05., Cross Roads J.4.d.10.85., Cross Roads
       D.29.c.80.40., Road Junctions D.30.b.30.80. – E.28.c.6.4.
       (b) Platoon Guides will await arrival of Unit at junction of
       FONQUEVILLERS – GOMME COURT ROAD with old enemy front
       line E.28.c.60.40. at 9.45 p.m. 21.5.18.
       Guides for Posts will meet Front Line Company "D" Coy. at
       Coy. HQ. K.5.d.60.80.

   (3) Order of Battle on taking over sector will be as follows:-
       Front Line Coy.   "D" Coy. 8th KLR. relieving "B" Coy. 9th KLR.
       Support   "   "C" "   "   "   "   "C" "   "   "
       Reserve   "   "B" "   "   "   "   "D" "   "   "
       Counter Attack " "A" "   "   "   "   "A" "   "   "

   (4)(a) One Officer and 4 N.C.Os. per Company, and one Officer
       and 2 N.C.Os. for Battalion HQ. already in the line will
       be responsible for taking over.
       (b) All maps, Defence Schemes, and particulars of work
       in progress or proposed will be carefully taken over.
       (c) Scheme of Defence and trench stores in present location
       will be carefully handed over and receipts obtained.

   (5) Relief Complete will be reported by wire using Code word
       "BERRY".

   (6) Battn. HQ. will close at present location at 7.30 p.m.
       21.5.18, and Rear HQ. will reopen at COUIN at that hour.
       Forward HQ. – head of column en route – opening at E.28.d.
       50.10. at 7.30 p.m. 21.5.18.

       Administrative Instructions have been issued to all
       concerned.

       ACKNOWLEDGE.

                                              Capt. & A/Adjt.
                                              8th (Irish) Batt. K.L.R.

Issued at 11.30 p.m.
Copies to:-
  1. 171 Inf. Bde.
  2. 9th KLR.
  3. C.O.
  4. 2nd-in-Command.
  5. Intell. Off. and LSO.
  6. Sigs. Off.
  7. – 11. 5 Companies.
  12. M.O.
  13. QM. and TO.
  14. R.M.
  15. File.
  16. War Diary.

8th (Irish) Battn. The King's (Liverpool Regiment)

8 Rivers — Army Form C. 2118.

WAR DIARY
INTELLIGENCE SUMMARY
(Erase heading not required.)

June 1918.

Place	Date 1918	Hour	Summary of Events and Information	Remarks and references to Appendices
Gonnecourt	1st June		Strength Effective 40 Off., 804 O.Rs. Ration 26 Off., 860 O.Rs.	
			Continuation of tour in front line — no operations of importance.	
			Casualties from 1st to 7th June Killed 1 Off. (2nd/Lt. R.H. Blake) 8 O.Rs. Died 1 Off.	
			(2/Lt. J. Morton) Died of wounds 1 Off. (2/Lt. H. Heysham) and 6 O.Rs. Wounded 31 O.Rs.	(1)
	7th June		Relieved in the left sub-sector of the right Brigade sector by the 25th Battn. King's	
			Own Royal Lancaster Regt. and marched out to camp in wood at Couin Ref.	
			57 D.N.E. J.1.6.	
	8th to 11th June		Cleaning up — bathing — Training — Saluting — Arms & Close order drill — Physical	
			Training &c.	
	11th June		Relieved 2/6th Battn. K.L.R. in Beer Trench & Chateau de la Haie. Order of	
			Battle Beer Trench A.Coy Right, B.Coy Left, Chateau C.Coy Right, D.Coy Left.	(2)
			Two Companies at the Chateau working at night in forward area.	
	14th June		Battn. (less one Coy (E Coy)) relieved 24th Battn. South Lancs Regt. in reserve to	
			the left Brigade sector. Order of Battle Right Coy A. Left Coy E. Julius Point	(3)
Louvain			D. P.Coy relieved F.Coy of the 9th Battn. K.L.R. in Christ Trench.	
			and came under Orders of 2/6th BN K.L.R. Commdg. 8th (Irish) Battn. K.L.R.	

P. F. Joss Major
Commdg. 8th (Irish) Battn. K.L.R.

Army Form C. 2118.

8th (Irish) Batt. The King's Liverpool Regt.

WAR DIARY
OR
INTELLIGENCE SUMMARY.
(Erase heading not required.)

June 1918.

Place	Date 1918	Hour	Summary of Events and Information	Remarks and references to Appendices
Somencourt	21st June		B Coy relieved in Chilli Trench and returned at Centre Coy in Reserve positions. All Coys working in forward areas each night - quiet tour, average activity of Enemy artillery. Casualties 1 Off (Lieut J.F. Wood wounded at duty) 4 O.R.'s Killed 16 O.R.'s wounded. (4 at duty)	(4)
	29th June		Relieved in Line by 24th Batt'n Royal North Lancs Regt, and came out to positions at Chateau de la Haie. Orders of Battle Right to Left A.B.C. & D Less 4 Lewis Gun Sections in positions in Bois French.	(5)
	30th June		Cleaning up. Strength Effective 38 Off & 901 O.R. Ration 20 Off & 658 O.R. The following drafts arrived during the month:- 11/6/18 49 O.R. 17/6/18 46 O.R. 19/6/18 51 O.R.	
	22 June		Major G. Jones M.C. assumed command of the Batt'n in the absence of Lt. Col. E. Heath D.S.O. (Kent Camp)	

J.G. Jones Major
Comm'g 8th (Irish) Batt'n K.L.R.

SECRET.   Copy No. 11

Operation Order No. 32.
8th (Serv) Bn. King's Liverpool Regt.
Ref Map:-
57D. NE 1/20,000.   ① 6/6/1918

1. This Battalion will be relieved by the
95th K.O.Y.L.I. Regt. in the left sub sector
of the Right Brigade on the night of
6th/8th June 1918.
"A" Coy 8th K.L.R. will be relieved by "A" Coy 75th KORLR
"B"   "   "   "   "   "   "   "B" "   "   "
"C"   "   "   "   "   "   "   "C" "   "   "
"D"   "   "   "   "   "   "   "D" "   "   "
Relief will commence about 10 p.m.

2. Guides. O.C. Coys will detail guides
as follows:-
1 per Platoon, 1 per Coy H.Q. & 1 for Bn. H.Q.
to be at Junc. of Mule Track and
FONQUEVILLERS — GOMMECOURT Road
(E.28.c.9.8.) at 9-30 p.m.
Guides for posts will be detailed
as follows:-
"A" Coy. – 1 per post at Junc. of BIEZ SWITCH
and GOMMECOURT TRENCH.
"B" Coy. – 1 per post at Junc. of FISH
ALLEY & GOMMECOURT TRENCH.

3. Trench Stores. 1 W.O. per Coy. of incoming unit will arrive during the afternoon to take over Trench Stores.
All maps, defence schemes, particulars of work in progress and proposed will be carefully handed over. Receipts will be forwarded to Bn. H.Q. by 3 p.m. 8-6-1918.

4. On Relief this Battn. will move by march route as under:—
H.Q. 'A' + 'C' Coys to COIGNEUX, J.9.a.
'B' + 'D' Coys to ROSSIGNOL FARM.
1 Guide per platoon to be detailed from personnel proceeding to Transport lines tomorrow morning will meet their respective platoons at the point where the Mule Track crosses the FONQUEVILLERS — SAILLY AU BOIS Road at 11-0 p.m. and guide the Battn. to billets.

5. Relief complete will be wired by the CODE WORD "RECEIVED".
On arrival at new positions Coys. will report to Bn. H.Q. by runner.

Sheet No. 3.

Battn. HQ. will close at present location on completion of Relief and reopen at CUIGNEUX at Midnight 7/8th June 1918.

Administrative Instructions have been issued to all concerned.

ACKNOWLEDGE.

Issued at 10pm.

W. Hornby.
2/Lt. sant adjt.
8th (Irish) Bn. K.L.R.

Copies to
1. 171st Inf Bde.
2. 75th K.L.R (Regt.)
3. OC A Coy
4. " B "
5. " C "
6. " D "
7. " HQ "
8. QM & TO.
9. Battn. in Left.
10. CO
11. OC Rear HQ.
12. Adjt.
13. War Diary.
14. File.

8th (IRISH) Battn. The King's Lpool Regt.
Administrative Instructions
with reference to O.O. 32.

(I) TRANSPORT — Camp Kettles, Mess Stores etc will be stacked at LONE TREE by 10.30pm. 2 men per Coy will remain at see Stores on limber. H.Qrs will stack Mess Box, B.O.R Box at H.Q Ration Dump by 10.30pm.
All Coy Lewis Guns, Trigger Spar G.A Bags (excepting 1 G) will be taken to LONE TREE after relief. Bags will be taken to H.Q Ration Dump.

(II) Cleanliness of Trenches
O.C Coys will see that the Trenches in their Sector are thoroughly clean & will obtain a Certificate to this effect from incoming Unit.

TRENCH STORES
(III) All Petrol Tins will be sent to H.Qrs as soon as possible after dusk. Water Tanks (1) & Petrol Tins (40) will be handed over full.

(IV.) The QM will arrange for Officers Valises to be taken to new positions during the afternoon. Breakfast will be served to Coys on arrival.

W. Hornby
/Lt & Asst Adjt

SECRET.   COPY NO 15

8th (IRISH) BATTALION. "THE KING'S" (LIVERPOOL REGT).

ADMINISTRATIVE INSTRUCTIONS
issued with Operation Order No 33.

10/6/18.

1. (a) Officers Valises, Packs, Coy and Orderly Room Stores, and all Kits not required for the Trenches, will be dumped in Battalion Dump by 1.0 p.m. 11/6/18. Field Kitchens will be ready to move by 2.0 p.m.
(b) Transport Officer will arrange to move these to Rear Headquarters in the early afternoon.
(c) All Stores for the trenches will be dumped in Battalion Dump by 2.0 p.m. 11/6/1918. Lewis Gun Limbers will be loaded and ready to move by 2.30 p.m. A & B Coys will man carry Lewis Guns from the LOUASTRE X FORK.

2. Dress for trenches. Officers, Slacks and Puttees and Officers S.D. Jackets, otherwise Fighting order. Other ranks, Fighting Order plus Greatcoats.

3. Trench and Area Stores, especially Hot Food Containers and Petrol Tins will be carefully taken over. Lists of Stores taken over will be forwarded to Battalion Headquarters by 9.0 a.m. 12/6/1918.

4. O.C. Coys will send down each night one pair of socks per man, and the Quartermaster will arrange to exchange these for clean ones which must be sent up each night by Ration Limbers.

5. Rations and Water will be brought up to the Chateau by 3.0 p.m. daily. For A & B Coys to ST MARTINS LANE DUMP at 10.0 p.m. each night.

6. The Camp at present location will be left in a clean and sanitary condition and will be ready for inspection by the 2nd in Command by 2.0 p.m. 11/6/1918. Clean certificates will be obtained.

7. Regimental Aid Post will be at B Coy, E.27.d.80.60.

Capt & Adjt.
8th (Irish) Bn. K.L.R.

Issued at 10.30 p.m.
By Runner
To all concerned.

SECRET

8th (IRISH) BATTALION "THE KING'S" (L'POOL REGT).
OPERATION ORDER NO 33.

Ref: 57 D. N.E. 1/20000.   10/6/1918

(1)   This Battalion will relieve the 2/6th (Rifle) K.L.R. in BEER TRENCH and CHATEAU DE LA HAIE on June 11th, 1918.

(2)   (a) The Battalion will move from present location in the order Hdqrs, A, B, C, D, Coys at 3.0 p.m. Platoons will move at 200 yards distance via Cross Roads J.7.B.70.64 – Road Junctions J.9.B.50.15 – Road Junction J.4.C.60.05 – CrossRoads J.4.D.10.85. – D.30.C.20.50 to CHATEAU.
        A & B Coys as above to J.4.D.10.85. thence Cross Roads D.29.C.80.40. – Road Junctions D.30.B.30.80 – E.27.B.1060. to BEER TRENCH.

        (b) Guides for Headquarters, C & D Coys will meet Platoons at N.E. corner CHATEAU at 4.0 p.m. Platoon Guides for A & B Coy Headquarters will meet Platoons at the junction of Mule Track and Fonquevillers Road and Sailly-au-Bois at 4.0 p.m.

(3)   Order of Battle on taking over will be as follows:-
BEER TRENCH.
Right Coy A Coy 8th K.L.R. relieving A Coy 2/6th K.L.R.
Left Coy B   "   "   "   "   B   "   "   "
CHATEAU.
Right Coy C   "   "   "   "   C   "   "   "
Left Coy D   "   "   "   "   D   "   "   "

(4)   (a) One Officer and 4 N.C.O.s and two Signallers per Coy – 2/Lt F.OPENSHAW, one N.C.O. two Signallers, and two Runners for Battalion Headquarters will parade at 10.30 a.m. at Battalion Orderly Room to-morrow and will proceed forward to take over.
        (b) All Maps, Defence Schemes, and particulars of work in progress and proposed will be carefully taken over.
        (c) Scheme of Defence and Area Stores in present location will be carefully handed over and receipts obtained.

(5)   Relief must be complete by 7.0 p.m. and will be reported by wire using the Code-word CAR.

(6)   Battalion Headquarters will close at present location at 3.0 p.m. 11/6/1918 and Rear Headquarters will re-open at COUIN at that time. Forward Headquarters will open at the CHATEAU DE LA HAIE at 3.0 p.m. 11/6/1918.

A C K N O W L E D G E.

                                              Capt & Adjt.
                                              8th (Irish) Bn. K.L.R.

Issued at 10.30 p.m.
By Runner.
Copies to :-
1. 171. Inf Bde.   2. C.O.   3. 2nd in Command.
4. Adjt.   5. H.Q.Coy. 6-9 A.B.C.D. Coys.
10. I.O.   11. T.O.   12. Q.M.
13. M.O.   14. R.S.M. 15. FILE.
16. War Diary.   17. O.C. Sigs.

SECRET.   COPY NO ......
                   8th (IRISH) BATTALION. "THE KING'S" (L'POOL R).
                                OPERATION ORDER NO.__

Ref. 57 D. N.E. 1/20,000.   ③   12/6/18.

1.   This Battalion, less one Coy (B Coy) will relieve
    the 2/4th S.Lanc.Regt, Reserve Battalion, Left Brigade
    Sector on the night 14/15th June, 1918.

2. (a)   H.Q. C & D Coys. will move from present location in
    order named at 5.30 p.m. 14/6/18.

    (b)   A Coy will move from their present location at
    6 pm 14/6/18.
    1/2 Platoons will move at 200 yds distance via MULE TRACK
    to junction of the FONQUEVILLERS - GOMMECOURT ROAD and
    MULE TRACK.

    (b)   Guides for HQrs, A, C, & D Coys will meet Platoons
    and Coy HQrs at junction MULE TRACK and FONQUEVILLERS -
    GOMMECOURT ROAD at 6.0 pm.

    (c)   B Coy will move from present location at 6.30 pm
    and take up position in SCOUT TRENCH at 9.45 pm. Guides
    will meet them in SCOUT TRENCH and they will move up to
    relieve B Coy, 9th Bn. K.L.R. On relief they will come under
    orders of O.C. 2/6th K.L.R.

3.   Order of Battle on taking over will be as follows :-

    Right Coy. (A Coy, 8th K.L.R.) relieving B Coy 2/4th S.LR.
    and Right half of A Coy, 2/4th S.L.R.
    Left Coy. (C Coy, 8th K.L.R.) relieving C Coy, 2/4th S.L.R.
    and Left half of A Coy, 2/4th S.L.R.
    JULIEN POINT. D Coy, 8th K.L.R. relieving D Coy, 2/4th S.L.R.

4. (a)   One Officer, 4 N.C.Os. and 2 Signallers per Coy, 2/Lt
    A.T.MICKLING, 1 N.C.O. 2 Signallers, & 2 Runners for
    Battalion HQrs will meet at junction of MULE TRACK and
    FONQUEVILLERS - GOMMECOURT ROAD at 2.30 pm and proceed
    forward to take over.

    (b)   All Maps, Defence Schemes, particulars of work in progress
    and proposed will be carefully taken over.

    (c)   Scheme of Defence and Trench Stores in present location
    will be carefully handed over and receipt obtained.

5.   Relief must be complete by 9.30 pm and will be reported
    by wire using the Codeword PIG.

6.   Forward Battalion HQrs will close at present location
    at 5.30 pm 14/6/18, and re-open at HUMSHPORT at that
    time. Rear Battalion HQrs will remain at COUIN.

    ACKNOWLEDGE.

                                                    (signed)
                                                    Capt & Adjt.
                                                    8th (Irish) Bn. K.L.R.
    Issued at H.Q. midnight.
    By Runner.
    Copies to :-
    1. 171 Bde.   2. Commanding Officer.   3. Adjt.
    4. O.C.Rear HQ.   5-9. A, B, C, D, HQ Coys.   10. T.O.
    11. Q.M.   12. M.O.   13. 2/6th K.L.R.
    14. 2/4th S.L.R.   15. 9th K.L.R.   16. R.E.
    17. Signals.   18. War Diary.   19. File.

SECRET   COPY NO ____

8th (IRISH) BATTALION. "THE KING'S" (L'POOL R.)
ADMINISTRATIVE INSTRUCTIONS ISSUED WITH OPERATION ORDER NO 34.

1. (a) Stores not required for trenches will be dumped at Batt H.Q. by 3.pm. T.O. will arrange to move same in the early afternoon.

   (b) Stores required for trenches will be dumped as follows:-
   A & B Coys on present Ration Dump.
   H.Q. C. & D Coys at Batt H.Q.
   Guards will be placed over these stores and T.O. will move to new locations at dusk.

   (c) Coys will man carry Lewis Guns and equipment.

2. Rations and Water for H.Q. A, C, & D Coys will come up about 10.0 pm to rear of STOUT TRENCH. The R.S.M. will arrange to have a Guide to point out the Dump to Transport. Coys will supply their own Ration carrying parties.

3. Q.M. and T.O. will at once arrange with the Q.M. and T.O. 2/6th K.L.R. re Rations and Water for B Coy, advising B Coy of the arrangements made and the location of the Dump.

4. O.C. Coys will send down each night one pair of socks per man, and the Q.M. will arrange to exchange these for clean ones; which must be sent up each night by Ration Limbers.

5. Trench & Area Stores, especially Hot Food Containers and Petrol Tins will be carefully taken over. List of Stores taken over will be forwarded to Battalion Hdqrs by 9.0 am 18/6/18.

6. O.C. Coys will obtain certificates that trenches have been left in a clean and sanitary condition.

7. R.A.P. will be in RUM SUPPORT as before.

Issued at 12.0 midnight.
To all concerned.

Capt & Adjt.
8th (Irish) Bn. K.L.R.

SECRET   Copy no 4

8th (IRISH) Bn. "The King's" (L'pool Regt).
Operation Order No 35

Map Ref:- 57D NE. 1/20,000   (4)   20/6/18

1/ "B" Coy, 8th K.L.R (Counter Attack Coy attached 2/6th K.L.R) will be relieved by "B" Coy, 2/6th K.L.R on the night 21/22nd June 1918.

2/ On relief "B" Coy, 8th K.L.R will withdraw to PURPLE LINE, taking over Centre position in GOMMECOURT SUPPORT & RUM TRENCH, & Coy H.Q at E.29.a.70.20.

3/ They will take over the two Right Posts from "A" Coy & the two Left Posts from "C" Coy, including Trench Stores for these Posts.
All arrangements to be made by O.C. Coys concerned.

4/ O.C "B" will send up 1 Officer for Coy & 1 N.C.O per Platoon to reconnoitre new positions before 2pm, 21/6/18.

5/ Defence Scheme, Maps & Trench Store Lists of Centre Coy will be carefully checked on taking over.

(cont)

Secret. Copy No 2

8th (Irish) Bn. "The King's" (L'pool R).
Administrative Instructions
issued with Operation Order 36
28/6/18.

1. (a) Coy Stores, Empty Patrol Tins, Officers Mess Kits, will be dumped at Battalion Ration Dump by 11.0pm 29/6/18. R.S.M. will detail Guard.
(b) Stores for BEER TRENCH will be man-handled under Coy arrangements.
(c) Coys will man-carry Lewis Guns and Equipment.

2. (a) Rations and Water for the Battalion (less 1 officer & 16 ORs) will be delivered to Chateau de la Haie before 10.0pm 29/6/18.
(b) Rations and Water for one Officer and 33 ORs "D Coy" will be delivered by Transport Officer to BEER TRENCH. Guide from "D Coy" will meet the Transport at the junction of the Mule Track and Fonquevillers - Gommecourt Rd at 10.30pm 29/6/18.
(c) CQMS and one Cook per Company will be included in forward parties and will arrange to make tea for the incoming Coys.

- 2 -

3. The Battalion R.A.P will be at Chateau de la Haie.

4. Trench and Area Stores, especially Hot Food Containers, Vermorel Sprayers, and Gum Boots will be very carefully handed over and receipts obtained; these & list Stores &c taken over at Chateau de la Haie and Bear Trench will be forwarded to Battalion Orderly Room by 9.0am 30/4/18. Coys will take special care in collecting and taking out all Battalion Patrol Tins.

5. All Dug-outs, and Coy Areas will be left scrupulously clean and Cleanliness certificate will be obtained.

6. Brigade HQ Gas Guard will be relieved by the incoming Unit by 12 noon 30/4/18 this Guard will report to Coy H.Q.

A.A.Sudbury
Capt & Adjt
H.O.N.I.

Issued at 8.0pm
By Runner to:-
1. C.O.   8. 2 in & T.O.   11. File.
2. Adjt   9. R.S.M.   12.
3-7. Coys. 10. War Diary.

-2-

(6) Relief must be completed by 2 A.M on 22/6/18, and will be notified by wire using the Code Word "GIN".

(7) O.C. Coys will send in revised dispositions by 12 Noon, 22nd June.

(8) Acknowledge.

[signature]
Capt & Adjt
8th (Irish) Battn. K.L.R.

20/6/18

Issued at
Copies to :-
1. 171st Infy Bde
2. C.O.
3. Adjt
4. O.C "B" Coy
5. 2/6th K.L.R
6. O.C "A" Coy
7.   "   "C" "
8. T.O. & 2.i/c
9. War Diary.

Headquarters.
52th Division.
. . . . .

> 8TH (IRISH) BN.
> "THE KING'S"
> (LIVERPOOL REGT.)
>
> No. 164
> Date.................

Herewith War Diary for the Month of
July, 1918.

                                    H. Cheske
                                    Lieut-Colonel,
            Commanding, 8th (Irish) Battn. K.L.R.

3.8.18.

Secret.   Copy No. 5
8th (Irish) Bn. "The King's" (L'pool R.)
Operation Order No. 36.

Ref 57. D. NE. 1/20,000.   ⑤   28/6/18.

1. This Battalion will be relieved by the 2/4th Loyal North Lancs Regt on the night 29/30th June, 1918.

2. On relief the Battalion will
(a) withdraw to the Chateau de la Haie.
(b) Dispositions as follows:-
Right Coy   A Coy 8th K.L.R taking over from D Coy 2/5th K.O.R.L.R.
Right Centre " B "   "   "   " C Coy "   "
Left Centre   " C "   "   "   " B Coy "   "
Left Coy   { D "   "   "   " A Coy "   "
             { less 4 L.G. Sections.

One officer (2/Lt F. L. Elsworth) and 4 Lewis Gun Sections D Coy will take over the position of permanent garrison in the Centre Coy area BEER TRENCH, relieving 4 L.G. sections C Coy 2/5th K.O.R.L.R.
(c) O.C. D Coy will arrange that this relief is completed by 9.45 pm.

3. (a) Advance parties of 4 N.C.O.s 1 Signaller, per Coy. 2/Lt H. Cheshire, 2. N.C.Os & 2 Signallers for Battalion

2.

Headquarters, will report at Chateau de la Haie at 3.30pm 29/6/18 and will take over.

(b) O.C. D. Coy will detail one Lewis Gun N.C.O to take over stores from C Coy, 2/5th K.O.R.L.R in BEER TRENCH, and 2/Lt Elsworth will reconnoitre this Area before 6.30pm 29/6/18. He will take over Defence Schemes and maps.

(c) All maps, Defence Schemes, particulars of work in progress and proposed will be carefully taken over.

(D) All maps, Defence Schemes, and Trench Stores in present locations will be carefully handed over and receipt obtained.

4. <u>Guides</u>. One guide per platoon, one guide for Coy H.Q. and one guide for Battalion H.Q. will meet incoming Unit at junction of Allsopps Trench and Gommecourt - Fonquevillers Rd, E.28.C.2.7 at 11.0pm 29/6/18. Guides will have written instructions, stating to which platoon they belong and whom they are to guide in.

-3-

5. Relief complete will be reported by wire, using the codeword "BLUE".

(b) Forward Battalion H.Q will close at present location at 12 midnight 29/30th June/18 and re-open at the Chateau de la Haie at that time.

Rear Battalion H.Q will remain at Couin.

Administrative Instructions have been issued to all concerned.

Acknowledge.

A A Carberry
Capt & adjt
HONI

Issued at 8pm
By Runner to:-
1. 171 Bde
2. 2/5 K.O.R.L.R
3. 2/4. L.N.L.R
4. C.O.
5. adjt
6-10. Coys
11. 2 m & T.O
12. R.S.M
13. War Diary
14. File.

SECRET.
8 Liverpool R

Army Form C. 2118.

8th (Irish) Battalion
"The King's" (Liverpool Regiment)

WAR DIARY
INTELLIGENCE SUMMARY.
(Erase heading not required.)

Vol 18

Place	Date	Hour	Summary of Events and Information	Remarks and references to Appendices
Chateau de la Haye Rf 57.D.N.E. T.6.b.	July 1st. 1918		Strength. Effective 38 Off. & 901 O.R. Ration. 20 Off. & 658 O.R. Relief by New Zealand Division in progress. This Battn vacated the reserve position round the Chateau de la Haye and marched out to camp in the Bois de Warnimont. Rf 57.D.N.W. I.18.c.0.4.	Appendix 1.
Bois de Warnimont	July 2nd to July 14th.		Division in Corps Reserve. Battalion under orders to move at 2 hours notice By day (9am to 9pm) 1 hours notice By night (9pm to 9am) 1 hours notice and occupy reserve positions in the red line and switch around Bus les Artois. Rf 57.D.N.E. I.36. During this period the men were allocated to intensive training of every nature - in addition Lectures & Classes for Officers & N.C.O's. Games & Sports. Reconnaissance by Officers & N.C.O's of parts of Corps front for counter attack if required.	18
HENU	July 15th.		Marched to HENU Rf 57.D.N.E. D.18.a. and took over billets lately occupied by a Battn of the 62nd Division.	
HENU	July 16th to Switch		Lieut. Col. E.B. Heath D.S.O. assumed Command of 174th Inf.Bde. the Command of the Battn is assumed by Major J.L. Jones M.C. Captain J.B. Brittain performing the duties of 2nd in Command of the Battn.	2.

Commandg. 8th (Irish) Batt. The King's (L'pool Regt)

SECRET

8th (Irish) Bn. K.L.R.

Army Form C. 2118.

WAR DIARY
INTELLIGENCE SUMMARY
(Erase heading not required.)

July 1918

Place 1918	Date	Hour	Summary of Events and Information	Remarks and references to Appendices
HENU	July 17th		Working Parties and Company Training. Lieut. W.G. Robinson reported for duty 12-7-18 and posted to "C" Coy	
HENU	18th		Lieut. A. Heyes, M.C. reported for duty 18-7-18, posted to "B" Coy	
HENU	16 - 28th		Training under Company Arrangements and Working Parties	Appendix 3
SUS-St. Leger	July 29th		Battalion moved to billets at SUS-St. Leger. Major J.F. Jones M.C. proceeded on Special Leave 28-7-18. Captain J.C. Smitham assumed command of Battn. 28-7-18	
ETRUN	30th		Battalion moved into Huts at ETRUN.	4
Trenches	31st		Battalion moves into Front Line trenches at FAMPOUX SOUTH SECTOR. Relieving 85th Bn. Canadian Infantry. BHQ St. B. H.15.b.4.0. Strength Effective 39 off. 937 o.r. Ration 28 off. 816 o.r. Casualties due to enemy action during the month Nil.	5
	July 31st		Lieut-Col. G.B. Heath S.O. resumed command of the Battn. and Captain J.C. Smitham resumed the duties of 2nd in Command	

T. G. B. Heath Lieut Colonel
Commanding 8th (Irish) Bn. K.L.R.

SECRET.   COPY NO. 16

8th (IRISH) BATTALION "THE KING'S" (L'POOL REGT).
OPERATION ORDER NO. 101.

Ref: 57D., NE., 1/20,000.
     57D., NW., 1/20,000.   1.7.18.

(1) This Battalion will move to Billets at BOIS de
    WARNIMONT, I.18.c.0.4. on July 2nd, 1918.

(2) Companies will move at 2.5 p.m. in the order HQrs, A,
    B, C, and D -200 yards distance between platoons, via
    Cross Roads J.6.b.25.80. - D.30.c.20.45. - thence by
    CHATEAU de la HAIE track to Road Junction J.4.c.95.20.
    , Road Junction J.4.c.55.00. - Road Junction J.9.b.
    50.18. - Cross Roads J.7.b.70.62. to BOIS DE WARNIMONT.

(3) "D" Company's Lewis Gun will be withdrawn from BEER
    TRENCH on the morning of 2.7.18 - movement to be by
    sections at 200 yards distance.   This move must be
    completed by 9 a.m.

(4) Trench Stores will be carefully checked, and list of
    same, together with Defence schemes, will be handed in
    to this Office by 10 a.m. 2.7.18.

(5) Arrival at new location will be notified to Battn. HQ.
    by Runner.

(6) Rear Bn. HQ. will move off from present location at
    1 p.m.   Details at MARIEUX will proceed direct to
    new location.

(7) Battn. HQ. will close at CHATEAU de la HAIE at 2.5 p.m.
    and will re-open at WARNIMONT at that hour.

    Location of Battn. HQ. - I.18.c.0.4.

    ACKNOWLEDGE.

Issued at 11.30 p.m.   Capt. & Adjt.
By Runner.   8th (Irish) Batt. K. L. R.
Copies to:-
  1. 171 Inf. Bde.
  2. C.O.
  3. O.C. Rear HQ.
  4 - 8. 5 Companies.
  9. Intell. and Sigs. Off.
 10. M.O.
 11. T.O.
 12. Q.M.
 13. R.S.M.
 14. File.
 15/16. War Diary.

-o-o-o-o-o-o-o-

SECRET. COPY NO. 16

8th (IRISH) BATTALION "THE KING'S" (L'POOL REGT).
ADMINISTRATIVE INSTRUCTIONS WITH
REFERENCE TO OPERATION ORDER 38.
-o-o-o-o-o-o-o-o-o-o-o-o-o-o-o-o-o-o-o-o-o-o-o-o-

1.7.18.

(1) Officers' Kits, Mess Boxes and Company Stores, Lewis Guns etc. will be dumped at Coy. HQ. by 1 p.m. HQrs. Valises and Orderly Room stores will be dumped at the CHATEAU de la HAIE at the same hour.
Only the minimum amount of movement is to be allowed in moving these stores.

(2) Rear HQrs. will be moved by Transport Officer as arranged with O.C. Rear HQ.

(3) Billets and trenches will be left scrupulously clean and will be ready for inspection by Capt. J.E. Smitham at 12 Noon.

(4) Lists of Trench and Area stores taken over in new area will be handed in to Battn. Orderly Room by 9 p.m. 2.7.18.

(5) The Quartermaster will arrange to have tea ready for Battn. on arrival at new billets.

Capt. & Adjt.
8th (Irish) Batt. K.L.R.

To all recipients of O.O.38.
(less Me.

SECRET.   COPY NO...
        8th(IRISH) BATTALION "THE KING'S"(L'POOL REGT).
                      OPERATION ORDER NO.39.
        -o-o-o-o-o-o-o-o-o-o-o-o-o-o-o-o-o-o-o-o-o-o-o-o-

Ref: Maps 57D.   ) 1/40,000.
           57D., NW.,) 1/20,000.
           57D., SW.,)   do.   14.7.18.

(1) This Battalion will move to Billets at HINU on 15.7.18.

(2) Companies will move off at 2.30 p.m. in the order,
    HQrs. A, B, C, and D, 200 yards distance between
    Platoons, via the track to fork roads I.12.d.95.05.
    thence road Junction J.1.d.42.78. COUIN - road
    Junction J.1.a.05.20. - fork road J.1.b.30.90. - road
    Junction D.19.b.25.12. HINU.

(3) Billeting Party of one Officer and 2 N.C.Os. per
    Coy., 2/Lt. Cheshire and 2 NCOs. for HQrs. will
    move off at 8.30 a.m. to meet Staff Captain, Town
    Major's Office, HINU, D.19.a.3.3. at 10 a.m.

(4) Guides will meet incoming Coys. at 3.45 p.m. road
    Junction D.19.b.25.12.

(5)(a) All maps, Defence Schemes in new location will be
       carefully taken over.
   (b) All Defence Schemes in present location will be
       handed in to Adjutant by 11 a.m. 15.7.18.

(6) Arrival at new location will be notified to Battn.
    HQrs. by runner.

(7) Battn. HQ. will close at WARNIMONT at 2.30 p.m. and
    reopen at HINU at that hour.

    A C K N O W L E D G E.

                                                    (signature)
                                                     Capt. & Adjt.
                                                     8th(Irish) Batt. K.L.R.

Issued at 10 p.m.
Copies to:-
    1. 171 Inf. Bde.
    2. C.O.
    3. 2nd-in-Command.
    4. Adjutant.
    5-9. Companies.
    10. Signalling Off.
    11. M.O.& L.G.O.
    12. T.O.
    13. Q.M.
    14. R.M.
    15. File.
    16. War Diary.
    17.   do.

SECRET. COPY NO. 15

8th (IRISH) BATTALION "THE KING'S" (LIVERPOOL REGT).
Administrative Instructions with reference to Operation Order No. 39.
-o-o-o-o-o-o-o-o-o-o-o-o-o-o-o-o-o-o-o-o-o-o-o-o-o-

14.7.18.

(1) (a) Officers' Valises, Coy. stores, Lewis Guns will be dumped by Church Army Hut by 11 a.m. 15.7.18.
 (b) Officers' Mess Kit will be dumped at same place by 2 p.m.
 (c) Field Kitchens will be ready to move by 1 p.m.
 (d) Petrol Tins will be dumped by Field Kitchens by 11 a.m. O.C. Coys. will ensure that no petrol tins are left in this area.

(2) Billets and Coy. areas will be left scrupulously clean, and will be ready for inspection by the 2nd-in-Command by 1 p.m. The usual clean certificate will be obtained, (from Town Major, AUTHIE) and forwarded to this Office by 8 p.m. 15.7.18.

(3) Tents will be left standing. The Quartermaster will hand these and area stores over to Town Major AUTHIE when he comes round, receipt and lists to be forwarded to this Office by 3 p.m. 15.7.18.

(4) One lorry will report to 2/6th KLR. at 6 a.m. This lorry will do 2 journeys for 2/6th KLR. who will then hand it over to 8th KLR. The Quartermaster will make necessary arrangements.

(5) SUPPLIES. Supply wagons will move full. Guides will meet Ration wagons at 3 p.m. Cross Roads D.19.b.2.4. Refilling for to-morrow, 15.7.18. remains the same, details regarding 16.7.18. will be notified later.

(6) O.C. "D" Coy. will provide a Guard of one NCO. and 3 men to take charge of Tents and Stores in this area, and one NCO. and 3 men for the Transport Lines. O.C. "D" Coy. will make necessary arrangements re rations. These men must be chosen from surplus personnel.

ACKNOWLEDGE.

[signature]

Capt. & Adjt.
8th (Irish) Batt. K.L.R.

Issued at 11 p.m.
Copies to:-
 1. C.O.
 2. 2nd-in-Command.
 3. Adjutant.
 4./8. Companies.
 9. Sigs. Off., LGO. and MO.,
 10. T.O.
 11. QM.
 12. RSM.
 13. File.
 14/15. War Diary.

-o-o-o-o-o-o-o-o-

SECRET.
Copy No. 12

8th (IRISH) BATTN. "THE KING'S" (LIVERPOOL REGT).
OPERATION ORDER No. 40.

Map Ref.
    57 D½, 1/40,000.
    51C., 1/40,000.

28.7.18.

(1) The Battalion will move to/Billets at SUS-ST-LEGER on 29.7.18.

(2) Order of March will be,
    Runners & Signallers.
    Band.   D   C
    HQrs., A, B, M, and M Companies.
The Battalion will parade in full marching order with the head of the column at Cross Roads D.19.a.50.30. (near Bn.HQ) ready to move, at 7 a.m.
Battn. will pass Brigade Starting Point at C.16.c.40.75. at 7.48 a.m.

(3) ROUTE. Route will be via PAS - MONDICOURT - Road Junction (T.11.c.8.0. NE. of LECHEUX) Cross Roads O.31.c.30.95.

(4) The following distances will be maintained between Units on march:-
    Between Companies ----- 100 yards.
    " Battn. & Transport 100 "

(5) Coy.Cdrs. will report in person when men are settled down in billets.

(6) All maps, defence schemes, in new location will be carefully taken over. All Defence Schemes in present location will be handed in to Adjutant by 6 a.m. 29.7.18.

(7) Battn.HQ. will close at present location at 8 a.m. Will be at head of column en route, and will reopen at SUS-ST-LEGER on arrival.

A C K N O W L E D G E.

H Cheshire

Lieut. & A/Adjt.
8th (Irish) Batt. K.L.R.

Issued at 11 p.m.
Copies to:-
1. 171 Inf. Bde.
2. C.O.
3. Adjt.
4/5 "A" Coy.
5. "B" "
6. "C" "
7. "D" "
8. HQrs. Coy.
9. QM.
10. T.O.
11. Sigs.Off.
12. File.
13/14. War Diary.
15. RSM.
16. M/O.

SECRET. COPY NO...

8th (IRISH) BATT. "THE KING'S" (LIVERPOOL REGIMENT)
ADMINISTRATIVE INSTRUCTIONS WITH
REFERENCE TO OPERATION ORDER 40.
=O=O=O=O=O=O=O=O=O=O=O=O=O=O=O=O=O=O=O=O=O=

28.7.18.

(1) <u>Billeting Parties.</u> One Officer per Coy. (including HQrs) will parade at B.O.R. at 6 a.m. and proceed to SUS-ST-LEGER. This party (of which 2/Lt. A.W. Hickling will be in charge) will report to Staff Captain at the Town Major's Office SUS-ST-LEGER at 10 a.m.

(2) <u>Baggage Wagons.</u> Horses for baggage wagons will report to transport lines tonight. On wagons passing No.3.Coy. 57th Div'l Train they will fall out and continue the march under the orders of O.C. No.3. Coy. 57th Div'l Train and rejoin Units on completion of the march. They will remain at the transport lines for the night.

(3) <u>Supplies.</u> Supply wagons will travel full. O.C. HQ. Coy. will arrange to have a guide at the Church, SUS-ST-LEGER at 2.30 p.m. Refilling will be at 7 a.m. to-morrow.

(4) <u>Lorries.</u> One lorry is allotted to this Unit for the moves for one journey only. The Q.M. will send a guide for this to present Brigade HQ. at 1.45 p.m. to-morrow.

(5) <u>Baggage.</u> All Officers' Kits, Packs and rifles of the band, Orderly Room stores, and mess boxes etc. will be delivered to Q.M. stores by 6 a.m. Loading party to be composed of light duty men to be detailed later. They will accompany lorry to new area.

(6) <u>Cleanliness.</u> All Billets and tents will be left in a clean and sanitary condition and a certificate to this effect will be handed in to Orderly Room by 8.30 a.m. O.C. "A" Coy. will inspect the quarters of "A" and "B" Coys. and O.C. "C" Coy. will inspect the quarters of "C" & "D" Coys. OC. HQrs. Coy. will inspect HQrs. Coy. billets.

(7) <u>Rear Party.</u> Rear Party, under 2/Lt. W. Hornby, consisting of one man from QM. stores and light duty men as per para. 5. Will hand over billets tents etc. and obtain usual certificates.

H. Cheshire.

Lieut. & A/Adjt.
8th (Irish) Batt. K.L.R.

Issued at 11 p.m.
Copies to all recipients of O.O. 40.

=O=O=O=O=O=O=O=

SECRET.

8th (IRISH) BATTN. "THE KING'S" (LIVERPOOL REGT).
OPERATION ORDER No. 41.

Copy No.

Reference Maps:-
1/40,000.

30/7/18.

1. The Battalion will move to Billets at ATHIES on 30.7.18.

2. Order of March will be :-
   Runners & Signallers, Band, H.Q., D, C, B & A Coys.
   The Battalion will parade in Battle Order with the head of the column at Road Junction M.04.a.70.20. at the Sothern end of the Village, ready to move at 9.15a.m.
   Battalion will pass Brigade Starting Point at 9.19.a.30.30. on the DUMBART-LIGNY - SOMBRIN ROAD at 9.35a.m.

3. ROUTE. Route will be Via BEAUMETZ-COURT - AVESNES and COURTE-BARBE.

4. The following distances will be maintained between Units on the march.
   Between Coys.   100 Yards.
   " Battn & Transport. "   "

5. Dinners will be served on the march, and will be ready by 12Noon.

6. Company Commanders will report in person when men are settled down in Billets.

7. All Maps, Defence Schemes etc in new location will be carefully taken over.

8. Battn. H.Q. will close at present location at 9.15a.m. - will be at head of column on Route - and will re-open at ATHIES on arrival.

H. Chesher

ACKNOWLEDGE.

Lieut & A/Adjt.
8th (Irish) Battn. K. L. Regt.

Issued at 3.30a.m.
Copies issued to:-

1. 171st Infy Bde.   8. H.Q. Coy.
2. C.O.   9. Q.M.
3. Adjt.   10. T.O.
4. "A" Coy.   11. Sigs. Officer.
5. "B" "   12. File.
6. "C" "   13. War Diary.
7. "D" "   14. "   "
                          15. M.O.
                          16. R.S.M.

-o-o-o-o-o-o-o-o-o-o-o-o-o-o-

SECRET   Copy No......
            8th (IRISH) BATTN. "THE KING'S" (LIVERPOOL REGT).
            ADMINISTRATIVE INSTRUCTIONS ISSUED WITH
                     OPERATION ORDER NO.41.   30.7.18.

1. **Billeting Parties:** One Officer per Coy (incl Hqrs) will
   parade at B.O.R. at 8.a.m. and proceed to XTRUIN. This
   party (of which 2/Lieut. A.W. Hickling will be in charge)
   will report to Staff Captain at Town Major's Office, XTRUIN
   at 1.30p.m.

2. **Baggage Wagons:** Baggage Wagons will march under the orders of
   O.C. No.3 Coy. 57th Divisional Train and rejoin units on
   completion of the march. They will remain at the Transport
   Lines for the night.

3. **Supplies:** Supply Wagons will travel full. O.C. H.Q. Coy.
   will arrange to have a guide at the Church, TRUIN at 4p.m.
   30th inst. Refilling was on the evening of the 29th inst.

4. **Lorries:** Three lorries are allotted to this Unit for the move for
   one journey only. The Q.M. will send a guide for same at
   Church, ..., at 1.45p.m. on 30th inst.

5. **Baggage:** All officers' Kits, Mess Packs, Rifles of the Band,
   Orderly Room Stores, Mess Boxes etc. will be dumped on the ground
   near Battn. Orderly Room by 9a.m. Loading party to be composed
   of Light duty men to be detailed later. They will accompany
   lorry to new area.

6. **Cleanliness:** All billets will be left in a clean and sanitary
   condition and a certificate to this effect will be handed in
   to B.O.R. by 8.30a.m.
   O.C. "A" Coy will inspect the quarters of "A" & "B" Coys.
   " "B" "   "   "   "   "   "C" " " "
   " "H" "   "   "   "   "   H.Q. Coy.

7. **Medical:** A Horse Ambulance will march in rear of the Battalion.

8. **Rear Party**, consisting of 2/Lieut. W. Horney, one man from
   Q.M. Stores and light duty men as per para 5. will hand over
   billets etc. and obtain usual certificates.

                                        Lieut & A/Adjt.,
                                  8th (Irish) Battn. K. L. Regt.

Issued at 3.30a.m,
   To all recipients of O.O.41.

        -@-o-@-o-@-o-o-@-o-@-o-@-o-@-o-@-

SECRET 16

HQ, 57th Division,

Herewith War Diary for this
Battalion for the month of
August 1918.

C. S. Heath
Lieut-Col,
Commdg. 1st (Rif) Bn Irish R.

5-9-18

SECRET.

8th Liverpool Regt

Army Form C. 2118

WAR DIARY
or
INTELLIGENCE SUMMARY.
(Erase heading not required.)

8th (Irish) Battn "The King's" (Liverpool Regiment)

August 1918

Place	Date 1918	Hour	Summary of Events and Information	Remarks and references to Appendices
			Effec Strength 39. Off & 937 OR. Ration Strength 28. Off & 816 OR.	
FAMPOUX Sheet 51B.	August 1.		Battalion holding Front Line of FAMPOUX SOUTH SECTOR. Order of Battle as follows:- Right Front. A. Coy. Left Front. B. Coy. Support C. Coy. Reserve D. Coy. Situation Quiet. No offensive action taken by the unit.	
		4/5	Inter-Company Relief. D Coy relieved A.Coy. C Coy relieved B. Coy. A+B Coys withdrew into new reserve positions in accordance with Provisional Defence Scheme.	(1)
	8/4		Battalion relieved by the 1/16th Rifle Batt: K.L.R. On relief the Battalion withdrew to Victory Camp. 51B. G.3.b.7.2. Casualties for the tour 1 OR. Killed. 5. OR. wounded.	(2)
Victory Camp	9		Battalion in Brigade Reserve. Reconnaissance of positions in accordance with Provisional Defence Scheme.	(3)
	10.		D. Coy went up to Railway Embankment S.E. H.14.a.05.30 and worked on defence positions on the 11th & 12th inst.	(4)
	13.		C. Coy relieved D. Coy and carried on with the work.	(5)
	9/5		Specialist Training & Company Training carried out	(6)

Cmmndg. 8th (Irish) Battn K. L. R.

8th (Irish) Batt. The Kings
(Liverpool Regiment)

WAR DIARY
of
INTELLIGENCE SUMMARY.
(Erase heading not required.)

SECRET.

Army Form C. 2118.

August 1918.

Place	Date 1918	Hour	Summary of Events and Information	Remarks and references to Appendices
	August 15/16		Relieved 2/4th Batt. K.O.R.R. as Support Batt. to the FAMPOUX SOUTH SECTOR. Order of Battn. A Coy. ATHIES, B Coy Railway Cutting C&D Coys Railway Embankment. Battn. H.Q. Railway Embankment. 51.B. H.13.d.90.90.	(7)
	16		2 Platoons of D. Coy move to Tilloy Trench H.8.a. + H.14.a. 9.2. Platoons of C. Coy move to Effie Switch South H.9.d.	
	18/19		Relieved by 6th Batt. Gordon Highlanders. Battn. withdrew to bivouacs at Anzin St Aubin 57.a L.12.a	(8)
	19		Entrained and moved to Monchy Breton Ry. Leus 11. 2.F. 30.80	
	20/21		Training of all Specialists & Company work.	
	21		Major J.Q. Jose M.C. returned from leave & resumed duties of 2nd in Command. Capt. J.B. Shuttam returned to the Command of D. Coy.	
	21		Marched to Izel-les-Hameau to billets N.21.	
	22		Marched to Gorgny to billets. 51.C.12.	
	23		Cleaning up. Inspection 7C.	
	24		Company & Battalion in the attack practised.	

C.J.O'Gilly
Lieut. Col.
Commdg. 8th (Irish) Batt. K.L.R.

SECRET.

8th (Irish) Batt:
The King's (Liverpool Regiment)

Army Form C. 2118.

WAR DIARY
and
INTELLIGENCE SUMMARY.

(Erase heading not required.)

August. 1918.

Place 1918	Date	Hour	Summary of Events and Information	Remarks and references to Appendices
	August 25th		B/Team went to Reinforcement camp at BARLY on the Evening of the 26th. Aug. 18. Batt: marched to GOUAY (Ref. Kew.II. H.15.95) and rested in billets One night.	
	26th		During the Evening the Batt: marched to Ground East of FICHEUX and bivouaced near Railway Embankment (Ref Shet 51.B. M7.27.a.)	
	27th		marched to ground East of MERCATEL and bivouaced for one night. vicinity M.30.a. Ref 51.B	
	28		marched to vicinity of St Martin our Cojeul (Ref 51.B.SW. N.33 central) and bivouaced for a few hours prior to moving up to positions in the Hindenburg Line in N.34.b. (Ref 51.B.SW) The Brigade was then in Divisional Reserve- the 172 Inf Bde had attacked that morning	
	29		Attack by the 170th Inf Bde. This Battalion moved forward. Line Report of situations up to MN 31/8/18 is attached.	
Casualties	28/31 Aug 1918		1 Off (Lt Robinson) wounded. 9. O.R. Killed. 52 O.Rs wounded	
Strength	31 Aug 1918		Eff: 47 Off. 885 O.Rs	
Ration			25 Off. 695. O.Rs	

D.J. Foott
Lieut Col
Commdg 8th (Irish) Batt: Kly Rgt

At 1p.m. on the 29.8.18. orders were received to move forward and occupy positions as follows:-

2 Companies in HOUP LANE - U.15.b.
2 " " USHER TRENCH - U.9.d.

This was in progress when verbal orders were given by B.G.C. 171st INFANTRY BRIGADE altering the dispositions to

2 Companies in CRUX TRENCH- U.9.c. & U.15.b.
2 " " COPSE TRENCH - U.8.d. & U.15.a.

supporting the flank facing N.E.

At 9pm. the same day when the Battalion was getting into position orders were given by the B.G.C., 170th INFANTRY BRIGADE (who had attacked that day) to send one Company on to the RIDGE between HENDECOURT & REINCOURT in U.17.b. & U.18.c. to link up to the Battalions holding these Villages and to assist in their defence against an enemy counter-attack. One of the Companies going up to COPSE TRENCH was detailed for this but at 10.39p.m. further orders were received from B.G.C., 170th INFANTRY BRIGADE to move the whole of the Battalion on to the RIDGE in U.17.b. & d. and U.18.c. to strengthen the line.

After this had been ordered Battalion H.Q. were established at U.8.b.40.60.

As no reports from Companies had been received by dawn of the 30.8.18. a personal reconnaissance of the forward area was made by made by the COMMANDING OFFICER and other Officers. It was then found that before this Battalion could reach the positions assigned to it in the last order the Village of REINCOURT was again in the hands of the enemy and that the forward position of our troops was on a line of the HENDECOURT-BULLECOURT ROAD and that our Companies had taken up positions in GUN ALLEY & POINTER ALLEY - &TRIDENT TRENCH (2 Companies), HOUP LANE (1 Company) and that the 4th Company which had been carrying ammunition - rations etc., from FONTAINE all night was getting forward.

At 8.30a.m. 30.8.18. word was received that the enemy were preparing to deliver a Counter-Attack from the direction of BULLECOURT. Immediately one Company was placed in position along HOUP LANE & COPSE TRENCH in U.15.a. & b. ready to fire due South across the VALLEY and up the forward slope toward BULLECOURT.

No enemy action followed but at 11a.m. an enemy operation was observed starting from REINCOURT - parties of the enemy moving towards our positions. These were engaged by all troops in the front line and the attack dispersed.

Between 1p.m. & 2p.m. parties of the enemy were seen in U.11.b. and U.12.a. & c. moving into HENDECOURT.

At 11a.m. all troops in the forward area were placed

under the command of LIEUT-COLONEL E.C. HEATH. D.S.O., the Commanding Officer of the 8th (IRISH) BATTN. "THE KING'S" (LIVERPOOL REGT.) with instructions to withdraw the whole of the remainder of the 170th INFANTRY BRIGADE and hold the then existing line with the 8th K.L.R. and 2/7th K.L.R. A Scheme of defence was drawn up and orders issued, disposing the 8th K.L.R. in front and the 2/7th K.L.R. in support on and behind the line "HOUP LANE".

At 5p.m. orders were received from the 171st INFANTRY BRIGADE that the line was to be held on a two Battalion Frontage with the 8th K.L.R. on the Right and the 2/7th K.L.R. on the Left. New dispositions were drawn up - orders issued and by 12 Midnight positions had been taken up and the 170th INFANTRY BRIGADE relieved. No Posts were handed over in the Village of HENDECOURT - the line on that flank running GUN ALLEY - SPANIEL ALLEY - HOUP LANE and CEMETERY AVENUE.

Battn. H.Q. were established at -

8th K.L.R. - U.9.a.30.60.
2/7th K.L.R. - U.9.a.40.15.

During the following day (31st August) Posts & Patrols were pushed forward on to BULLECOURT - HENDECOURT ROAD and up that part of TRIDENT ALLEY in U.16.b. and U.17.a. Touch was gained with the Division on the Right at the FACTORY.

At 10p.m. on the 31.8.18. orders were received for the 171st INFANTRY BRIGADE attack on the following morning.

SECRET.   Copy No. 8.

8th (IRISH) Battn. "The King's" (Liverpool Regt).
OPERATION ORDER No. 43.

Ref.
Sheet. FEUCHY. 1/10,000.
51. B. N.W. 1/20,000.   4.8.18.

1. An Inter-Company Relief will take place on the night 4th/5th August. 1918.

2. "D" Coy. (Reserve) will relieve "A" Coy. (Right Front)
   "C" " (Support)   "   "   "B" " (Left Front)

3. On relief "A" Company will move into Reserve Position vacated by "D" Company. and "B" Company will move into positions vacated by "C" Company in EFFIE TRENCH & CAROLINE TRENCH.

4. Relief will commence at 9.30p.m. Details as to guides etc. will be arranged by O.C. Coys.

5. 1 Officer of "A" Coy. and 1 Officer of "B" Coy. will remain in their present area with the relieving Coys. until after "Stand Down" on the morning of 5th Aug. 1918.

6. All Trench Stores. Maps. Defence Schemes and particulars of work will be handed over carefully.

7. Relief Complete will be reported by wire using the following Code Words :-

        "A" Company.   "PAPERS RECEIVED"

        "B"   "   "WATER ARRIVED"

        "C"   "   "IN HOSPITAL"

        "D"   "   "LAST WEEK"

ACKNOWLEDGE.

           2p.m.
Issued at 11.30a.m.   Lieut & A/Adjt.,
   Copies to :-   8th (Irish) Battn. K.L.R.

       1. 171st Inf. Bde.
       2. C.O.
       3. "A" Company.
       4. "B"   "
       5. "C"   "
       6. "D"   "
       7. Sigs. Officer.
       8. War Diary.
       9. "   "
      10. File.
      11. O.C. "B" Coy. 2/6th K.L.R. (for information)
      12. T.O.&.M.

SECRET.   COPY NO. 18

8th (IRISH) BATTN. "THE KING'S" (LIVERPOOL REGT.)

DEFENCE SCHEME - (PROVISIONAL)

FAMPOUX SOUTH SECTOR.
=o=o=o=o=o=o=o=o=o=o=o=o=o=o=o=o=o=o=o=o=o=o=o=

Ref. Map. 51.B. N.W. 1/20.000.
and Secret Map. FEUCHY. 1/10.000.   8.3.18.

1. **ENEMY.**	1.	The enemy is holding a line, approximately North and South, astride LA SCARPE RIVER, which, flowing East, cuts the line, South of FAMPOUX, at right angles. On the Left Bank his front line passes through the Eastern portion of FAMPOUX, but on the Right (South) Bank his line is 1.500 Yards further East than on the North. LA SCARPE RIVER forms a Divisional Boundary in the enemy's distribution.
2. **POSITION OF BRIGADE.**	2.	The 171st Infantry Brigade holds the FAMPOUX SOUTH SECTION of the Divisional Front and is the Centre Brigade of the Division. The 170th Infantry Brigade is on the Right and the 172nd Infantry Brigade on the Left.
3. **LINES OF DEFENCE & DISTRIBUTION OF TROOPS.**	3.	The Battalion occupies the First, or Green, system of the Sector, which consists of :-

       Main Outposts Line. - Pudding & Lemon Trenches

       Main Line. - Carolina & Dec Trenches.

and is responsible for the Outposts of the Sector. One Battalion is allotted to the Second, or Red, (TILLOY) system and one is held in Reserve.

4. **OUTPOST LINE.**	4.	The Outpost Line extends along LA SCARPE RIVER from H.22.a.75.35. to FAMPOUX - thence along STOKE TRENCH to PAT TRENCH (incl.) The Outpost System extends back to & includes the " MAIN OUTPOST LINE". The Outpost Area is divided into 2 Sub-Sectors - RIGHT (SCARPE & FAMPOUX) and LEFT (STOKE) each held by one Company. Each Coy. is on a front of two Platoons, with two Platoons in Support on the MAIN OUTPOST LINE. The flank support platoons each supply a liaison Post with Units on the flanks :- that on the Right at - H.22.a.75.35. that on the Left. - H.11.c.80.90.
5. **BOUNDARIES.**	5.	The Sector is bounded on the Right by LA SCARPE RIVER and on the Left by a line drawn from the Junction of PAT TRENCH with the front line, H.11.c.80.45. (inclusive) - Junction of CAMERON LANE with DEE TRENCH. H.11.c.-8.5.(incl) Junction of CAM AVENUE with EFFIE SWITCH SOUTH H.15.a.70.98. (exclusive) The dividing line between the two Sub-Sectors is; a line drawn from the Junction of STOKE Tr and Road at H.17.d.10.70. (incl. to Right Coy). junction of road and CAM AVENUE at H.17.c.10.70 (incl. to Left Coy.)- junction of PORT AVENUE TRENCH and CAM AVENUE - junction of PUDDING Tr and CAM AVENUE (inclusive to Right Coy) - junction of CAM AVENUE and CAROLINA TRENCH (incl. to Right Coy.) along CAM AVENUE to the junction with the CAM VALLEY at H.15.b.50.30. (all inclusive to the Right Company)

-2-

SYSTEM OF DEFENCE.

6. The system of Defence of the MAIN OUTPOST LINE is that of a series of defended localities forward of which is a line of section, and Double Section Posts.
These Posts are furnished by two Platoons of each of that two forward Companies, each of which platoons keeps one section in immediate support along the general line of STOKES SUPPORT. The remaining two Platoons of each Company are allotted to the 4 localities :-

    PEPPER.   PUDDING-PORT.
    CAM.   DEMON-LOGIC.

The 2 MAIN LINE and Reserve Companies have each two Platoons in the MAIN LINE and two in Reserve. those in the MAIN LINE being responsible for the areas - CAROLINA ½ - CAROLINA-COSSACK --- CAROLINA-EFFIE --- CAROLINA-DEE.
The Reserve Platoons of the Right Company are accommodated in COSSACK TRENCH, those of the Left in CAM VALLEY. They will be under the orders of the Senior Platoon Officer who will take up his quarters in CAM VALLEY.

7. ACTION IN THE EVENT OF ATTACK.

7. Should there be indications of an impending attack, the order "MAN BATTLE POSITION" will be given.
On receipt of this order Forward Posts of the Front Coys. will be withdrawn into the line of defended localities named in para. 6.
As soon as these parties have crossed the General line STOKES SUPPORT, the Garrisons of that line will take up the role of Active Patrols whose duty will be to impede the advance of the enemy and to report his movements.
The Battalion Reserve (4 Platoons) of 2 Platoons from each of the MAIN LINE Coys., will "STAND TO" in CAM VALLEY.
They will be available to reinforce the CAROLINA-DEE LINE, to form Defensive Flanks, or to Counter-attack if the line of Defended localities should be penetrated.
All other troops will man their Battle Positions.
All Battle Positions will be held to the last.
In the event of an attack coming as a surprize the above arrangements will all be carried out, except that no attempt will be made to withdraw the Forward Posts.

8. AMMUNITION.

8. There is a Reserve Supply of Ammunition at each Coy. H.Q. and one at Battn.H.Q.

9. COMMUNICATION.

9. (a) To Brigade.
    (i) By Fullerphone.
    (ii) By Power Buzzer & Amplifier. (also to Right & Left Battns.)
    (iii) Pigeons.
    (iv) Visual. By Lamp & Shutter from Ridge East of Battn.H.Q. to Bde Transmitter
    (v) By Runner & Cyclist Via Relay Post at H.15.a.05.10.
(b) Forward.
    By Fullerphone to Coys. in the line and Support on Buried route.
    By Runner to Reserve Coy. and Coys. in the line.
    By telephone from Right & Left Coys. to Forward Posts in HAMPOUX & STOKES TRENCH.

SECRET. COPY No. 9.

8th (IRISH) BN. "THE KING'S" (L'POOL REGT.)

PROVISIONAL DEFENCE SCHEME
-o-o-o-o-o-o-o-o-o-o-o-o-o-o-o

9.3.18.

AMENDMENT - No. 1

Reference Para. 2.(b) add :-

1 Platoon from "A" Coy. & "B" Coy. will be earmarked to come under orders of O.C. "S" Battalion. if required.

[signature]

Capt & Adjt.
8th (Irish) Battn
K.L.R.

To all recipients of P.D.S.

-3-

10. **MEDICAL ARRANGEMENTS.**	10.	The R.A.P. is situated at H.15.b.35.15. with an Advanced Dressing Station at H.14.b.5.2.
11. **HEADQUARTERS.**	11.	Headquarters are as follows :-

Battalion H.Q.   - H.15.b.3.0.
Right Front Coy.   - H.15.d.10.80.
Left   "   "   - H.16.b.70.80.
Right Reserve Coy.   - H.15.c.98.90.
Left   "   "   - H.15.b.40.30.

12. **REPORT.** 12. All reports to Battalion Headquarters.

13. **A C K N O W L E D G E.** 13.

[signature]

Capt & Adjt.,
8th (Irish) Battn. K.L.Regt.

Issued at 7pm..
    Copies to :-

1. 171st Inf. Bde.
2. C.O.
3. Adjt.
4/8. 5 Companies.
9. M.O.
10. S.O.
11. T.O.
12. T.O. & Q.M.
13. Centre Group Artillery.
14. 57th Div. M.G. Battn.
15. 171st L.T.M.B.
16. Right Battn.
17. Left Battn.
18/19. War Diary.
20. File.

-o-o-o-o-o-o-o-o-o-

SECRET.   COPY NO. 14.
          8th (IRISH) BATT. " THE KING'S " (LIVERPOOL REGIMENT).

                         OPERATION ORDER No. 44.

Ref. Map 51.b. N.W. 1/20.000.   7.8.18.

   (1) This Battalion will be relieved in the Front Line of the
       HAMROUX SECTOR (SOUTH) by the 2/6th (Rifle) Batt. K.L.R.
       on the night of the 8/9th August 1918.
       "D" Coy. 8th K.L.R.(Right Front) will be relieved by "D"
                                    Left Front   Coy. 2/6th K.L.R.
       "C" "   "   (Right Reserve) will be relieved by "C"
                                    Right Reserve Coy. 2/6th K.L.R.
       "A" "   "   (Left Reserve) will be relieved by "A"
                                    Coy. 2/6th K.L.R.
       "B" "   "   (Left Reserve) will be relieved by "B"
                                    Coy. 2/6th K.L.R.

       Relief will commence about 10.30p.m.

   (2) On relief the Battn. will withdraw to VICTORY CAMP by
       Light Railway, where they will be in Brigade Reserve.
       Companies will move to siding at N.1.d.6.4. as relieved
       and report to Lieut. J.F. Worrall who will be entraining
       Officer. Detraining point will be at ST. CATHERINE and
       from there Coys. will move by march route to VICTORY
       CAMP. The following distances will be maintained on
       both marches:-
               100 Yards between Platoons.
               500   "   "   Coys.

   (3) Advance Parties. All C.Q.M.S. will proceed by ration train
       to Transport Lines on night of 7th August 1918. to
       prepare Camp.
               1 Off. and one N.C.O. per Coy. will parade
       at Battn. Orderly Room at 9a.m. on 8.8.18. and will move
       to VICTORY CAMP to take over Maps, Defence Schemes etc.
       They will act as Guides to Companies from detraining point
       at ST. CATHERINE to Camp.

   (4) Guides. One per post for 2 front Coys. and one for Coy H.Q.
       Two per Platoon for 2 rear Coys. and one for Coy.H.Q.
       and two for Battn. H.Q.
       will meet Incoming Unit at BATHING Cross Roads N.15.a.00.0.5.
       at 10.15p.m. Guides will have written instructions stating
       to which post or Platoon they belong and whom they are to
       guide in.

   (5) Relief Complete will be reported by wire using the Code
       words as follows :-
               "A" Company.   REPORT SENT.
               "B"   "   ANGLE WON.
               "C"   "   VERY GOOD.
               "D"   "   NO LEAVE.

   (6) All Maps, Defence Schemes, particulars of work in progress
       or proposed, trench stores etc. will be carefully handed
       over, receipts for same, in duplicate, being sent to Bn.H.Q.
       by 9a.m. 9.8.18.
       Trenches, Dugouts, etc, will be left in a clean and sanitary
       condition, and a certificate to this effect, in duplicate
       will be forwarded to B.H.Q. by 9a.m. 9.8.18.

   (7) Administrative Instructions have been issued to all concerned.

       ACKNOWLEDGE.

                                              Capt & Adjt.,
                          8th (Irish) Battalion. K.L.Regt.

Issued at 10p.m.

Copies to :-

1. 171st Inf. Bde.
2. 2/6th K.L.R.
3/7. 5 Coys.
8. C.O.
9. Adjt.
10. Q.M.
11. T.O.
12. M.O.
13/14. War Diary.
15. File.
16. R.L.M.

-o-o-o-o-

SECRET. COPY NO. 4
8th (IRISH) BATT. "THE KING'S" (LIVERPOOL REGT)
ADMINISTRATIVE INSTRUCTION WITH
REFERENCE TO OPERATION ORDER 44.
-o-o-o-o-o-o-o-o-o-o-o-o-o-o-o-o-o-o-o-o-o-o

7.8.18.

(1) Coy. stores. Officer's Mess Kit, Medical Stores. Orderly Room Stores and all Petrol Tins not taken over as Trench Stores will be sent to Dump at the foot of CAM VALLEY H.16.d.00.50. by 10p.m. ready for removal by Transport.

(2) Rations, Lewis Gun Limbers, Mens Packs and Officers' Valises will be sent to VICTORY CAMP.

(3) The Quartermaster will arrange to have Tea ready on arrival of the Battn. in Camp.

(4) Men acting as Bde. Bomb Storemen will be relieved by 12 Noon. on 8.8.18.

(5) All surplus and 33% personnel will rejoin the Battn.

Capt. & Adjt.,
8th (Irish) Battn. K.L.R.

Issued to all recipients
of O.O. 44 (excepting Bde.)

SECRET.	COPY NO. 10

8th (IRISH) BATTN. "THE KING'S" (LIVERPOOL REGT.)

ADMINISTRATIVE INSTRUCTIONS ISSUED WITH
PROVISIONAL DEFENCE SCHEME.

9.3.18.

On receipt of the order "MAN BATTLE POS-ITION."

1. Companies (less "B" Team) will fall in on Company Alarm Posts in "FIGHTING ORDER".

2. Lewis Gun Limbers will proceed with Companies.

3. Unexpended portion of days rations will be carried by all ranks.

4. Officers' Valises, Packs and Coy. Stores will be dumped by Battn. Orderly Room. O.C. "B" Coy. will detail Guard of 1 N.C.O. & 4 men from "B" Team to take charge of these stores. The Quartermaster will arrange to move stores to Transport Lines.

5. Field Kitchens will be returned to Transport Lines.

6. Water Bottles must always be kept full.

7. "B" Team will come under the command of the senior "B" Team Officer, who will be responsible for clearing the Camp and obtaining clean Certificates before moving off to Divisional Reception Camp.

A O Carberry

Capt & Adjt.,
8th (Irish) Battn. K.L.Regt.

Issued at 9.15p.m.
To all recipients of P.D. Scheme.

SECRET.
COPY NO....

8th (IRISH) BATTN. "THE KING'S" (LIVERPOOL REGIMENT)

OPERATION ORDER NO.45.a

-o-o-o-o--o-o-o-o-o-o-o-o-

Map. Ref. 51. B. N.W. 1/20.000.
12.8.18.

1. On the morning of August. 13th. 1918. "C" Company will relieve "D" Company in the RAILWAY EMBANKMENT.

2. Advance Party of 1 Officer & 4 N.C.Os. will move up on night 12th/13th. August. to take over billets.

3. Relief will commence at 1.30a.m. 13th August. "C" Coy. moving up by March Route by Platoons at ½ Hour intervals. 1st Platoon to move from VICTORY CAMP at 11p.m. Aug. 12th.

4. Lewis Gun Limber will proceed with "C" Company. Transport Officer will arrange to collect Officers' Valises, Coy. Stores etc. and send up with rations.

5. "D" Company will move down to ST CATHERINES by train at 2.30a.m.

6. "D" Company Field Kitchen will remain at Embankment and will be taken over by "C" Company.

7. "D" Coy. Stores, Officers' Valises will be returned by rail to ST CATHERINES and Transport Officer will move same so from there to VICTORY CAMP.

8. Detail of Work will be carefully handed over by "D" Coy.

9. Relief complete will be wired to Brigade Headquarters & Battn. H.Q. using the Code Word. "ROSE".

Capt. & Adjt.,
8th (Irish) Battn. K.L.R.

Issued at 12.40p.m.
Copies to :-

1. 171st Inf, Bde.
2. C.O.
3. 2nd-in-Cd.
4. Adjt.,
5. O.C. "C" Coy.
6. " "D" "
7. Quartermaster.
8. Transport Officer.
9/10. War Diary.
11. Cpl. Bebbington. "D" Coy.
12. File.

-o-o-o-o-o-

SECRET.   COPY NO. 14.

8th (IRISH) BTTN. "THE KING'S" (LIVERPOOL REGIMENT).

OPERATION ORDER NO. 44a

=o=o=o=o=o=o=o=o=o=o=o=o=o=o=o=o=o=

Ref. Map 51. B. N.W. 1/20.000.   14.8.18.

1. This Battalion will relieve the 2/7th Battalion
    "The King's" (Liverpool Regt.), Support Battalion,
    Centre Brigade (FAMPOUX SECTOR) on the night of
    the 15th/16th August 1918.

2. (A) The Battalion (less 1 Coy.) will move from present
    location at 8.30p.m. by March Route in the order -
    Hdqrs - A - B - D Coys. - 100 Yards interval
    between Platoons and 500 Yards between Companies;
    via ST CATHERINES - ST NICHOLAS - ST LAURENT BLANGY-
    RAILWAY EMBANKMENT.

   (B) Guides for A - B & D Coys. will meet incoming Coys.
    at Embankment at 9.30p.m. 15.8.18.

   (C) O.C. "C" Coy (Railway Cutting) will relieve "C" Coy.
    2/7th K.L.R. before 9.30p.m., arrangements to made direct
    with O.C. Coy. concerned.

3. Order of Battle on taking over will be as follows:-

    ATHIES   "A" Coy. 8th K.L.R. relieving "A" Coy. 2/7th.KLR
    RAILWAY ("B"   "   "   "   "   "B" "   "
    EMBANKMENT ("C"   "   "   "   "   "C" "   "
             ("D"   "   "   "   "   "D" "   "

4. (A) Advance Parties of 1 Officer - 1 N.C.O. and 2 Signallers
    per Coy. and Lieut. H. Cheshire - 1 N.C.O. and 2
    Signallers for Bttn. H.Q. will parade at B.O.R. at 11am.
    15.8.18 and move to the Embankment to take over.
    They will assist in guiding incoming Coys. to their
    positions.

   (B) All Maps, Defence Schemes and particulars of work in
    progress and proposed will be carefully taken over.

   (C) Schemes of Defence and Area Stores in present
    location will be carefully handed over and receipts
    obtained.

5. Relief Complete will be reported by wire using the
    Code Word " JAM ".

6. (A) Bttn. H.Q. will close at present location at 8.30pm.
    15.8.18. and will re-open at Railway Embankment at
    the same hour.

   (B) Rear Hdqrs will re-open at WAVERLEY CAMP at 8.30p.m.
    15.8.18.

A C K N O W L E D G E.

                                                    R A Carbery
                                                    Capt & Adjt.,
                                                    8th (Irish) Bttn. K.L.Regt.

Issued at 9p.m.

Copies to :-

1. 171st Infantry Brigade.
2. Commanding Officer.
3. Adjutant.
4. O.C. "A" Coy.
5. "   "B" "
6. "   "C" "
7. "   "D" "
8. "   H.Q. "
9. T.O. & Q.M.
10. M.O.
11. 2/7th K.L.R.
12. L.G.O.
13. 2nd-in-Command.
14. War Diary.
15. "   "
16. File.
17. R.S.M.

-o-o-o-o-o-

SECRET.   COPY NO.

8th (IRISH) BATTN. "THE KING'S" (LIVERPOOL REGIMENT).

ADMINISTRATIVE INSTRUCTIONS ISSUED IN
ACCORDANCE WITH OPERATION ORDER NO. 44a

–o–o–o–o–o–o–o–o–o–o–o–o–o–o–o–o–o–o–o–o–o–o–o–

14.8.18.

          Room
1. (a) Coy. & Orderly Stores. Packs and all Kits not required
for the line will be dumped in Coy. Dumps by 3p.m. 15.8.18.

  (b) Coy. & Orderly Room Stores, Officers' Valises & Kits etc.,
required for the line will be dumped in Company Dumps by
7pm. 15.8.18.

  (c) Field Kitchens will not be taken up the line.

  (d) Lewis Gun Limbers will proceed with Companies.

2. (a) 2/Lieut. A.W. Hickling will be i/c of Rear Hdqrs personnel
& will act as Asst. Adjt., and will remain at Rear Hdqrs.

  (b) "B" Team will parade at 7.30p.m. at Battn. Orderly Room
under 2/Lieut. H. Boothman. and report to Reinforcement
Camp carrying 24 Hrs rations.

3. (a) List of Area Stores handed over will be forwarded in
duplicate to Battn. H.Q. by 6p.m. 15.8.18.

  (b) List of Trench & Area Stores taken over will be forwarded
in duplicate to Battn. H.Q. by 10a.m. 16.8.18.

                    up
4. Rations will be brought by Light Railway on the 15th &
preceeding nights. Those for "A" Coy. being dumped at
STORE DUMP, balance at Embankment. All CQM. will be
up with Rations on the 15th inst.

5. Quartermaster will make necessary arrangements re Socks.

6. The Camp at present location will be left on a clean &
sanitary condition and will be ready for inspection by
2nd-in-Command by 5p.m. 15.8.18. Clean Certificates
will be obtained.

                                      A. Canberry

                                  Capt & Adjt.,
                           8th (Irish) Battn. K.L. Regt.

Issued at 3p.m.

  Copies to all concerned.

8" Liverpool.

September

1918.

10/6991

50th Division

1/4th Northumberland Fus^rs
Vol III
Sep^t. 15.

8th (Irish) Battn. The Kings
(Liverpool) Regt.

SECRET.   Army Form C. 2118.

WAR DIARY
an
INTELLIGENCE SUMMARY.
(Erase heading not required.)

S Liverpool Rgt 171/57

September 1918.

Place	Date	Hour	Summary of Events and Information	Remarks and references to Appendices
Havrincourt Sheet 51.B. U.16.	1st Septr.		Strength. Off. 47 O.R. 1885 O.R. Ration 25 Off. 9695 O.R. Successful attack by A & D Companies - Full report to be attached of all operations up to the 3rd Sept: also had following ground captured and consolidated. Casualties 13rd Sept. 5 O.R. Killed, 22 O.R. wounded	① 98 20 20+
Sheet 51.B. U.15.6.	4th Septr. 7th Septr.		Re-organization of Companies and cleaning up. Relieved the 1st Battn. Artists Rifles on Right Front Battn of the INCH Sector Order of Battle Right Front. C. Coy. Support. A. Coy. Battn. H.Q. at Left front. B. Coy. Reserve. D. Coy. 57. C. E. 7.C. 05. 00.	②
	8th Septr.		Active patrolling of Enemy posts which were always found to be very alert - with M.G. activity both by day & night. Enemy artillery active especially at dawn. Several gas & blue cross bombardments.	
	11th Septr.		In conjunction with flank troops an attack was made to establish our front line along the Canal du Nord. This was unsuccessful but on our right the village of MOEUVRE was captured.	③
	12th Septr.		Counter attack on the Village of MOEUVRE attacked. A full detailed report of these two days to be attached. On the morning of the 12th Septr. Major JG Jones M.C. assumed command of the Battn: Lieut Col (A/Lt) Meath D.S.O. who had been evacuated (Sick)	④

8th (Irish) Battn. The Kings (Liverpool) Regt.

SECRET.

Army Form C. 2118.

WAR DIARY
of
INTELLIGENCE SUMMARY.
(Erase heading not required.)

September 1918.

Instructions regarding War Diaries and Intelligence Summaries are contained in F.S. Regs., Part II. and the Staff Manual respectively. Title pages will be prepared in manuscript.

Place	Date	Hour	Summary of Events and Information	Remarks and references to Appendices
INCHY.	13th Sept.		On the morning of the 13th Sept. the relief of the Battn by the 1st Battn Royal Munster Fusiliers. This Battn withdrawing to positions in Sheet 51.B. V.27.a. South of Cagnicourt.	(5)
	13/6 Sept. 17th do.		Brigade in Div Reserve. Re-organization, cleaning up &c. Relieved by 1/4th Battn Royal Scots and moved by march route to positions in 51.B. T.30.6. where Battn bivouaced for the night. Casualties for tour in line. 3 Off. killed 6 Off. wounded. 21 O.R. killed, 98 O.R. wounded 10 O.R. missing.	(6)
	18th do		Battn moved by train to billets at SOMBRIN. Sheet 57.c. O.23. Entraining at BOYELLES detraining at LATHER LIÉ RE.	(7)
SOMBRIN.	19/24 do		Re-organization of Battn. Platoon, Company & Specialist Training. Tactical Schemes &c.	(8)
	25th do.		Battn. moved by train to bivouac area in D.13.a. Sheet 57C NE. S.W of Queant.	
Queant.	27. Sept 2.0 am		Active Operations commenced a full report up to including the 30th Sept. is attached.	(9)
	30. Sept		Strength Effective - 39 Off & 690 O.R., Ration 24 Off & 700 O.R.	

Jno. Dizzy Erace? E.
Major
Commdg 8th (Irish) Battn The Kings (Liverpool) Regt.

This Battalion's objective was a line TERRIER TRENCH at Road at U.22.b.85.40. and GREYHOUND TRENCH to the HENDECOURT - RIENCOURT ROAD at U.17.a.70.10. Orders were issued for the attack on a two Company Front with MORDEN TRENCH as the dividing boundary.

Companies were disposed with two Platoons of each in Front and two Platoons in Support.

ZERO was at 4.50a.m. and four minutes later the front Platoons moved off from the line GUN ALLEY following the barrage across open country toward their objective - the direction of attack being S.E.

With the exception of of M.G. fire from S.E. Corner of HENDECOURT little opposition was met until reaching objective. The enemy counter Artillery barrage being slight and distributed.

The objective trench was found to be well manned with M.Gs. This was reached by 5.10a.m. and several hand to hand encounters with the enemy ensued.

A Platoon worked up TERRIER AVENUE beyond its junction with GREYHOUND TRENCH and established a block at its junction with MORDEN TRENCH.

At 6.30a.m. it was reported that the whole of this system was in our hands and the garrison either Killed or Captured.

Patrols were sent out to establish liaison with troops on flanks - At 8.30a.m. touch was gained with the 2/7th K.L.R. at the junction of GREYHOUND TRENCH and HENDECOURT TRENCH and at 11.30a.m. touch was gained with the 52nd DIVISION at BULLDOG

Number of Prisoners captured during the operation - 60 (approx.) and 12 Machine Guns.

The work of re-organisation and consolidation was carried on during the morning with little interference from the enemy.

From 4p.m. onwards the 2/6th K.L.R. assembled on our objective and at 6.5p.m. went forward to attack RIENCOURT.

At 8.30p.m. a Patrol was sent forward to get in touch with them and it was found they had occupied the Village and had gained and were consolidating the objective in EMU TRENCH.

This operation made this Battalion in support to the 2/6th K.L.R. and close liaison was kept with them and with the flanks during the night.

On the morning of the 2nd September operations were carried out by troops on Left and Right which did not effect this Unit and the same dispositions were kept. Battn. H.Q. at U.15.b.35.20.

At 10.35a.m. on 3.9.18. orders were received to withdraw our troops from present dispositions and concentrate the Battn. in positions in U.15.b. This was completed at 4p.m.

Throug out the operation the Artillery preparation and support was excellent. The initial barrage on the morning of the 1st Sept. could not have been better.

J. Fitzgerald Jones
Lieut-Colonel,
Commanding, 8th (Irish) Battn. K. L. Regt.

3.9.18.

SECRET.   8th (IRISH) Bn. "THE KING'S" (LIVERPOOL REGT.)   COPY No.....
OPERATION ORDER No. 47

Ref. Maps:-   7.9.18.
Sheets 51B & 57C (1/40,000)

1. (a) This Battalion will relieve the 1st Battn. ARTSTS' RIFLES.
    Right Front Battalion, 190th Infantry Brigade (INCHY
    SECTOR) on the night of 7th/8th September 1918.

   (b) The 2/7th K.L.R. will be on the left with Battn. H.Q.
    at D.6.d.50.15.

   (c) The 2/6th K.L.R. will be in Reserve with Battn. H.Q.
    at D.6.d.20.40.

   (d) The 1st SCOTS' GUARDS will be on the Right.

2. (a) The Battalion (less Rear H.Q. and "B" Team) will move
    from present location at 3p.m. by March Route in the
    order :-
            H.Q. - "C" - "B" - "A" - "D"
    300 yards distance between Coys., overland route to
    HENDECOURT - RIENCOURT ROAD - thence RIENCOURT -
    CAGNICOURT.

   (b) Battalion will halt at V.15.d. S.E. of CAGNICOURT where
    tea will be served, moving from that point at 7.30p.m. in
    same order as in para. 2(a) Platoons at 100 Yards distance,
    Via CROSS ROADS V.21.b.60.45. - CROSS ROADS V.28.b.42.95.
    thence to ROAD JUNCTION D.6.d.95.30.

   (c) Guides of one per Platoon and Coy. H.Q. and one for Battn.
    H.Q. will meet incoming Coys. at D.6.d.95.30. at 8.30p.m.

3.   Order of Battle on taking over will be as follows :-
         Right Front "C" 8th KLR. relieving "A" Coy ARTISTS' RIFLES.
         Left   "   "B" "   "   "D" "   "   "
         Support.   "A" "   "   "B" "   "   "
         Reserve.   "D" "   "   "C" "   "   "

4. Advance Parties - 1 Officer. 2 N.C.Os. 2 Runners & 1 Signaller
   (a) per Coy. and Capt. J.F. Wormall. 2 N.C.Os. 2 Runners & Signallers +
    2 Runners will parade at B.O.R. at 9a.m. and move to
    line to take over, meeting guide at D.6.d.95.30. at
    11.30a.m.

   (b) All Maps, Defence Schemes, particulars of work in
    progress and proposed will be carefully taken over.

5.   Dress :-   Fighting Order.

6.   Rear H.Q. and "B" Team will parade in the VALLEY near
    Transport Lines at 4p.m. and move off to C.6.d. under
    the command of Major. J.F. Jones. M.C.

7.   Relief Complete will be notified by wire using the code
    Word " NIL ".

8. (a) Battn. H.Q. will close at present location at 3p.m.
    7.9.18. and re-open at the same hour at D.18.b.90.90.

   (b) Rear H.Q. will open at C.6.d. at 5p.m. 7.9.18.

9.   A C K N O W L E D G E .

                                            Capt & Adjt.
                                            8th (Irish) Battn. K.L.R.
Issued at 1p.m
   Copies to:-
      1. 171st Inf. Bde.   2. C.O.   3. 2nd-in-Cd.
      4/8. 5 Companies.   9. T.O.   10. M.O.
     11. Sigs. Offr.   12/13. War Diary. 14. File.

SECRET.   COPY NO...

8t (Irish) Battn. "THE KING'S" (LIVERPOOL REGT.)
ADMINISTRATIVE INSTRUCTIONS ISSUED IN
ACCORDANCE WITH OPERATION ORDER No. 47.

-o-o-o-o-o-o-o-o-o-o-o-o-o-o-o-o-o-o-o-o-o-o-o-o-

1. Orderly Room and Coy. Stores, Officers' Valises, Packs,
   (a) Trench Shelters and all Kits not required for the line
       will be dumped at Q.M. Stores by 1p.m. 7.9.18.

   (b) Stores for the line, which must be cut down to a minimum
       will be dumped at Q.M. Stores by 2p.m. 7.9.18.

   (c) Field Kitchens will move with Coys. to V.15.d. and will
       return to Transport after Tea.

   (d) Lewis Gun Limbers will move with Coys. to Road Junction
       D.6.d.95.30.

2. Quartermaster will make necessary arrangements re Socks.

3. The Camp, Latrines etc., at present location will be left in
   a clean and sanitary condition.

4. Transport Officer will arrange to bring up the dump of
   S.A.A. & Bombs at present location to Battn. H.Q. at
   D.12.b.90.90.

5. Rear H.Q. and Transport Lines will come to C.6.d.

6. R.A.P. will be in the INDYSBURG LINE SUPPORT - D.12.d.85.20.

7. The 16 Auxiliary Stretcher Bearers will parade under 2/Lieut.
   F.S. Knowles at B.Q.R. at 1.30p.m. 7.9.18. and report to
   Bearer Officer at 2/2nd Wessex Field Ambulance at 171st
   Infy. Bde.
   They will carry 3 Days Rations.

8. WATER.
           Well at Battn. H.Q. at D.6.d.80.20.
            "   " R.A.P. near 2/7th K.L.R. H.Q.

           These must be treated before use.

                                                    [signature]
                                                    Capt. & Adjt.,
                                                    8t (Irish) Battn. K.L.R.

Issued at 1p.m.
    Copies issued to all concerned.

SECRET.　　　　　　　　　　　　　　　　　　　　　　　　COPY NO. 10.

8th (IRISH) BATTN. "THE KING'S" (LIVERPOOL REGT.)

PROVISIONAL DEFENCE SCHEME.
-o-o-o- -o-o-o-o-o-o-o-o-o-o-o-o-o-o-o-o-o-o-o-

Ref. Map. 51. B. N.W. 1/20.000.　　　　　　　　　　9.8.18.

1. During the time the Battalion is in this Area it will be in Brigade Reserve and will be prepared to move at one hours notice before "SUNSET" to "SUNRISE". Transport need not be loaded.

2. On receipt of the order "MAN BATTLE POSITION" Companies will move forward by selected routes to positions of assembly as under :-

   (a) Battn. H.Q. to the Railway Cutting.
   (b) "A" & "B" Coys. to the positions vacated by the two Coys. of the Support Battn. on the Railway.
   (c) "C" & "D" Coys. to BLANGY TRENCH in G.12.d. & G.18.b.

3. On arrival in these positions the Battalion will be prepared to act as follows :-

   (a) Battn. H.Q. - A & B Coys. to reinforce the Second System (TILLOY TRENCHES) if necessary.

   Keeping in touch with the situation on the North of the Brigade Boundary in the SECOND SYSTEM & stopping the enemy turning the Northern Flank, or making a gap in the line.

   (b) "C" & "D" Coys. under the Command of the Senior Company Commander :-

   To deny enemy entering MUSKETRY VALLEY from the Northern End.
   To move to TILLOY RESERVE.
   To reinforce the Second System (TILLOY TRENCHES)

   (c) The whole of the Battalion may be required to restore the situation on any part of the front, or flanks, in the event of the enemy having pierced same, and when the situation has been sufficiently cleared up to enable a successful Counter-attack to be launched. This would normally be launched with Artillery preparation from the line of the Railway.

4. All Battle Positions will be held to the last.

5. All positions of assembly and various routes to same will be reconnoitred forthwith by all Officers.

　　　　　　　　　　　　　　　　　　　　　　Capt & Adjt.
　　　　　　　　　　　　　　　　　　　8th (Irish) Battn. K.L.Regt.

Issued at 4.15p.m.
　Copies to :-

　　1. C.O.
　　2. Adjt.
　　3. I.O.
　　4/8. 5 Coys.
　　9/10. War Diary.
　　11. File.
　　12. S.O.
　　13. Q.M. & T.O.

SECRET.   8th (IRISH) BATTN. "THE KING'S" (LIVERPOOL REGT.)

OPERATION ORDER NO. 46.

=o=o=o=o=o=o=o=o=o=o=o=o=o=o=o=o=o=o=

COPY No. 18

Ref. Map. 51.44.B. 1/40.000.   17.8.18.
"   "   51.51.B & C. 1/40.000.

1. (a) This Battalion will be relieved as Support Battn. Centre Brigade. (FAMPOUX SOUTH SECTOR) by the 6th GORDON HIGHLANDERS. on the night of the 18th/19th. August. 1918.

   (b) "A" Coy. 8th K.L.R. (ATHIES) will be relieved by "A" Coy. 6th Gordons.
       "B" "   "   "   (RAILWAY CUTTING)   "   "   "   "B" Coy. 6th Gordons.
       "C" "   "   "   (2 Platoons EMBANKMENT.)   "   "C" Coy.
                          (2   "   ENFIL SWITCH SOUTH) 6th Gordons.
       "D" "   "   "   (2 Platoons TILLOY TRENCH.) "   "D" Coy.
                          (2   "   EMBANKMENT.)   6th Gordons.

   (c) Relief will commence about 10.30p.m.

2. (a) On Relief the Battalion will withdraw by March Route to Bivouacs at ANZIN - 200 Yds Distance between Platoons - 500 Yds between Coys. - Via ST LAURENT BLANGY - ST NICHOLAS - ST CATHERINE - ANZIN.

3. (b) The 2nd-in-Command will arrange site for Bivouacs and Guides to meet the Battn. at Cross Roads - G.1.d.60.00. at 12 Midnight 18th/19th. August.

3. ADVANCE PARTIES.   Capt. J.F. Worrall - 1 N.C.O. for Bn. H.Q. 1 N.C.O. for "A" & "B" Coys. - 1 N.C.O for "C" & "D" Coys. 1 N.C.O. for Q.M. Stores & Transport will report at Town Majors Office ANZIN-ST.AUBIN at 8a.m. Aug. 18th. and proceed by Motor Lorry to MONCHY BRETON as billeting party.

4. GUIDES. (a) 1 Guide per Coy. will report at Brigade H.Q. G.18.b.3.2. at 2p.m. 18.8.18. to meet and guide advance parties 6th Gordons to their respective Coy. H.Q.

   (b) One Guide per Platoon and Coy. H.Q. will meet incoming Unit at Bridge - H.14.a.05.40. at 10pm.
       Guides will have written instructions stating which Platoon they belong to and which they are to guide in.

5. (a) All Defence Schemes, Maps, Aeroplane Photos, particulars of work in progress and proposed, trench stores etc., will be carefully handed over, receipts for same in duplicate being sent to Battn. H.Q. by 8p.m. 18.8.18.

   (b) Camps, Horse Lines, Trenches, & Dugouts will be left in a thoroughly clean & sanitary condition, (O.C. Coys. will be responsible for their Coy. Areas, Lieut. F.A. Hoare for Hdqrs - 2/Lieut. R.T. Simpson. M.C., for Transport and 2nd-in-Command for the whole of Rear H.Q.) and a Certificate to this effect will be obtained from relieving Unit and sent to Battn. H.Q. by 8p.m. 18.8.18.

6. Relief Complete will be reported by wire using the Code Word - "PEPPER".

7. The Battn. will entrain at ARTILLERY CORNER (L.12.a.) for MONCHY BRETON at about 6a.m. 19.8.18. Coys. will move from ANZIN in the order - Bn.H.Q.,A,B,C, & D Coys. at 5a.m. Distance as in para 2., reporting to entraining Officer (Lieut. H. Cheshire).

8. Transport will move by road as per attached March Table.
   "B".

SECRET. COPY No. 18

8th. (IRISH) BATTN. "THE KING'S" (LIVERPOOL REGT.)

ADMINISTRATIVE INSTRUCTIONS ISSUED IN
ACCORDANCE WITH OPERATION ORDER No. 46.

-o-o-o-o-o- -o-o-o-o-o-o-o-o-o-o-o-o-o-

17.8.18

1. (a) Orderly Room, Coy & Medical Stores, Officers' Trench Bundles, Dixies, Petrol Tins etc., will be sent to Dump at Junction of Embankment & Road (H.14.a.05.40) by 8p.m. 18.8.18

   (b) Officers' Mess Boxes, by 9.30p.m.
   The R.Q.M. will be responsible for the Dump.

   (c) O.C. Coys. will ensure that Lewis Guns are loaded on limbers as quickly as possible, these limbers will proceed with Coys. to ANZIN, joining the Transport Convoy on the 19th.

2. The 2nd-in-Command will arrange for Breakfast for Officers and men at ANZIN, about 4a.m. 19.8.18.

3. Haversack Rations including Tea Rations will be carried by all ranks, on the 19th inst., and will not be eaten until ordered.
   The Quartermaster will arrange that Dinner is served at MONCHY about 3p.m. to 4p.m.

4. All Duties except Brigade Guard will be relieved by 6pm. 18.8.18.

5. One Lorry is allotted to this Unit to assist on Move. The Quartermaster will arrange to send a Guide to Town Majors Office, ANZIN-ST-AUBIN at 2p.m. Aug. 18th to meet same.

6. Mens' Packs, will be issued out before moving from ANZIN. The Quartermaster will arrange for these to be placed in Coy. Dumps ready for distribution.

A. Canbury
Capt & Adjt.,
8th (Irish) Batt. K.L.R.

Issued at 9pm.

Copies to all concerned.

9. Battn. H.Q. will close at present location on completion of Relief 18th/19th August. 1918, and will re-open at Rear. H.Q. at the same hour until 5a.m. 19.8.18., thence head of column reopening at MONCHY BRETON at 12 Noon August 19th. 1918.

10. Administrative Instructions issued to all concerned.

ACKNOWLEDGE.

Capt & Adjt.,
8th (Irish) Bn. K.L.Regt.

Issued at 9p.m.
Copies to :-

1. 171st Inf. Bde.
2. C.O.
3. 2nd-in-Cd.
4. Adjt.,
5/9. 5 Coys.
10. M.O.
11. Sig. Officer.
12. Intell. Officer.
13. Transport Officer.
14. Quartermaster.
15. Works Officer.
16. Rear H.Q.
17. R.S.M.
18/19. War Diary.
20. 6th Gordons.
21. File.
22.
23.

-o-o-o--o-o-o-o-o-o-

PRELIMINARY REPORT ON OPERATION EAST AND
SOUTH EAST OF INCHY - 11.9.18.

1. Attack upon various points of CANAL DU NORD was made on a two Company front ("C" Coy. on Right and "B" Coy. on left) with one Company ("A" Coy.) in Support and one Coy ("D" Coy) in Reserve. Assaulting Companies attacked on the following frontages:-

   Right Coy. Two Platoons with an additional section attached to each Platoon for mopping up.

   Left Coy. Three Platoons with one Section attached to each Platoon for mopping up.

   Coy. delimitations and objectives are shewn on attached sketchings.

2. The barrage opened at 6.15p.m. but was very sketchy from E.8.c. to Right Boundary. It was discovered on barrage lifting and our troops moving to the assault that the barrage had entirely missed Machine Guns which were located in :-

   (1) Continuation of HOBART STREET about 100Yds E. of Road.
   (2) In the CABLE TRENCH about 80 Yds East of Road;
   (3) At a point about 100 Yds to Right of (2).
   (4) About 10 Machine Guns in E.8.a. & c.

   The Right Company met with heavy Machine Gun & Rifle fire immediately after leaving our lines and was held up - both Officers becoming casualties, in addition to heavy loss amongst N.C.Os. and men. The Right Coy. Commander at once pushed another Platoon forward to press the attack, but this failed to make any progress in face of heavy fire.

   The Left Coy. met with slightly better success, No.5 Platoon pressed on to the CANAL and captured No.3 Post. (E.8.d.62.40.) establishing themselves on the Eastern Embankment. The Platoon had now been reduced to 1 Officer & 5 Other Ranks and as Platoons on the Right and Left had failed to come up, after holding on for about half an hour they withdrew to the jumping off position. The remaining two Platoons of this Coy. which were operating on the left and centre of Coy. frontage were held up by tremendous fire from about 10 Machine Guns in trees in E.8.a. & c. These Machine Guns were dealt with one by one until the Platoons had been so reduced so as to make further progress impossible. - they were withdrawn to jumping off positions.

3. At about 12 Midnight the Reserve Coy. ("D" Coy) endeavoured to push two Platoons along HOBART TRENCH and two Platoons along CEMETERY SUPPORT with a view to establishing Posts at E.14.b.8.5. - @ E.14.b.7.9. - E.3.d.6.4. - E.8.a.9.2. - This Coy. moved up within a 100 Yds of the CANAL where it was met by heavy M.G. fire & T.M. fire from the Eastern Embankment - the Coy. pressed forward to within 40 Yds of the CANAL but found position untenable and retired to our original position, having suffered heavy casualties.

4. The Battalion is now being reorganized - original positions have been re-established and are held as follows :-

   Right Front : - "C" Coy. plus 1 Platoon "A" Coy.
   Left   "   :- "B" "   "   3   "   "A" "
   Support.   :- "D" Company.
   Reserve.   :- 1 Company. 2/6th K.L.R.

   A defensive flank has been formed along general line of CEMETERY SUPPORT from our Right Post at E.14.a.48.10. to E.14.d.98.10. by 2/6th K.L.R. We are in touch with 2/7th K.L.R. on left on original lines.

   Captain A/Adjt. Major,
   Commdg. 8th (Irish) Battn. K.L.Regt.

14.9.18.

Headquarters.
171st Infantry Brigade.
-o-o-o-o-o-o-o-o-o-o-o-o-o-

In continuation of my report of 11.9.18. on operations E. & S.E. of INCHY I have to give the following additional information.

(1). CASUALTIES.   The Casualties sustained by this Unit were as follows :-

Officers :- Killed. 3   Lieut. A.D. Gibson.
                         2/Lieut. A. Steel.
                         "   J.F. Lee.

            Wounded. 6. 2/Lieut. A. Cookson.
                         "   A.A. Olley.
                         "   G.S. Nicholas.
                         "   E. BOULFIELD.
                         "   H. Irwin; M.C., M.M.
                         "   A.E.A. Booth.

2/Lieut. H. Irwin., M.C., M.M. has since returned to duty.

Other Ranks :-   Killed.   Wounded.   Missing.
                 16.   70.   13.

(2) PRISONERS.
Thirteen Prisoners were taken and delivered to Prisoners Cage.

(3) CORRECTION.
The Statement that a Post was established on Eastern Embankment of CANAL-du-NORD in para. 2. of my previous report would appear to be incorrect.   The Post was established at M.8.d.6.6.   Some notes on Canal Defences are attached.

(4) GALLANT SERVICE.

I have to call your attention to the gallant service of the undermentioned Officers :-

1. Major. A.H. Falkner. R.A.M.C. (T)
2. Lieut. F.T. Edwards.

The former did exceptionally good work in tending and evacuating the wounded. Owing to the unexpectedly large number of casualties it was found that the process of bringing down wounded to the Aid Post for treatment was too slow; Major Falkner thereupon moved to the forward area and personally organized the work of collection from "No Man's Land" and evacuation, in addition to dealing with their wounds.
He displayed great gallantry and coolness in this service under very heavy shell & machine gun fire.

The latter displayed exceptional gallantry and coolness.   When he found that his Platoon was suffering heavily from Machine Gun fire from front and flanks he led his men into a trench (WARCBURG TRENCH) and pressed on to his objective.   When he arrived there although his Platoon was reduced to five men and no other troops on his right or left had gained the objective he fought the position for thirty mins. inflicting casualties upon the enemy who was assembling for counter-attack.   When he found that he was in danger of being outflanked he

Report on CANAL-DU-NORD at a point 57C. N.E. - E.8.d.6.6.

-o-o-o-o-o-o-o-o-o-o-o-

On approaching CANAL from WEST a thin line of wire and an old Light Railway is crossed. You then climb a gradual slope up the bank which is about 15 Feet high at this point, with a crest about 4 Feet wide.

The dry basin of the CANAL is about 25 Feet wide with almost perpendicular sides 20 Feet high.

The Eastern Bank has a similar crest with a gradual slope away from the CANAL which rises again as the ground approaches the CANAL-DU-NORD TRENCH. This Trench is strongly held by Machine Guns which command both banks of the CANAL.

In the basin of the CANAL at this point is a red brick building about 12 Feet square which contained parties of the enemy. Several small concrete Pill-boxes were also noticed in the CANAL basin SOUTH of this point.

Headquarters.
171st Infantry Brigade.
-o-o-o-o-o-o-o-o-o-o-o-o-o-

Report on Enemy Operations against MOEUVRES 12.9.18.

8.30p.m. — O.C. "C" Coy. JONI reported to me that a trench on his Right Front had been taken by enemy which was confirmed a moment later by my O.C. Centre Coy.

8.35p.m. — 2/Lieut. BRUTT of "A" Coy. JONI reported personally at Battn. H.Q. and stated that the enemy had attacked their positions in CEMETERY SUPPORT — that his company had retired together with troops of RED BRIGADE — that the enemy were in MOEUVRES — that his Company Commander had been severely wounded and that he was unable to indicate the positions to which his company or troops on right flank had retired.

I immediately ordered this Officer to return to his Company and to re-organise it in CEMETERY SUPPORT in area E.19.c.90.75. to E.14.c.40.90. gaining touch on left with Right Platoon of my Centre Company which was holding its original position.

I ordered O.C. "C" Coy. JONI to establish blocks in HINDENBURG LINE SUPPORT at E.13.d.56.25. and E.14.d.7.5. — thus refusing the flank — and to push out patrols in E.14.a. & E.14.d. to locate enemy and establish touch on right — also to ensure touch with "A" JONI by pushing Patrol up CEMETERY SUPPORT.

I ordered my Support Coy. to hold one Platoon in readiness to Support Centre Coy — which was rather weak.

9p.m. — Reported this to Bde H.Q. and O.C. JONI — asking O.C. Battn. on Right for his situation and giving him my own.

9.30p.m. — O.C. "C" Coy. JONI. reported that new position had been taken up and that he was in touch with RED BDE at Junction of CEMETERY SUPPORT and HINDENBURG SUPPORT.

10.30p.m. — Received message from Bde that MAGNUM was sending fighting patrols to clear village and occupy CEMETERY SUPPORT from E.14.d.7.5. westwards. O.C. "C" Coy. JONI informed and instructed that Patrols and Posts previously ordered to gain touch with MAGNUM Posts when established.

11.20p.m. — Received attached report from O.C. 1/5th L.N.L.Regt. (1)

2.35a.m. — Received attached report from O.C. 1/5th L.N.L.Regt. (2)

5a.m. — Relief complete — dispositions handed over as per attached sketch map.

Major,
Commanding, 8th (Irish) Battn. K.L.Regt.

14.9.18.

Headquarters.
   171st Infantry Brigade.
-o-o-o-o-o-o-o-o-o-o-o-o-o-

I have questioned 2/Lieut. TEBBUTT re withdrawal from CEMETERY SUPPORT positions last night. He states that he saw men falling back through MOEUVRES and that he then saw an Officer whom he took to be his Company Commander blowing a whistle and giving the signal for "retire". He withdrew with his men towards the road running from E.14.c.4.0. to E.8.c.25.00.where he met the other Officer of his Company, 2/Lieut. HARPER, who told him that the Company Commander had been seriously wounded. He then came down to Battn. H². and on being ordered by me to reform his Company and re-organise, went forward and established Posts as per enclosed sketch & map, from which it will be observed that they were behind our line. I heard from the O.C. my Centre Coy. that these remnants passed between our No.1 & No.2 Posts (Centre Coy.) whilst the withdrawal was on. I have been unable to question 2/Lieut. HARPER. So far as can be ascertained all men of this Coy. who are not casualties are now out of the trenches.

J. Fitzgerald Jones
Major,
Commanding, 8th (Irish) Battn. K. L. Regt.

14.9.18.

SECRET   "JOSLI"   Copy No. 10
Operation Order No. 49
11/9/18.

1. (a) At ZERO hour – which will be 6.15pm to-night Sept 11/12th – The 141st Infy Bde will advance its line to the general line of the Canal Bank.

(b) 8th K.L.R. will be on the Right
    2/7th   "   "   "   "   "   Left.

(c) The 1/5th L.N.L.R. will be on the Right of 8th K.L.R.

2. At ZERO the 8th K.L.R. will move forward to the line CANAL BANK E.15.a.00.00 – E.8.b.30.50. establishing Platoon Strong Posts as under:-

      E.14.b.93.35
      E.8.d.62.40
      E.8.d.35.80
      E.8.b.30.35
      E.14.b.80.95

3. "C" Coy will be on the Right & will capture & consolidate Strong Posts

      E.14.b.93.35.
      E.14.b.80.85.

-2-

"D" Coy will be on the Left & will
capture & consolidate :-
      E.8.d.62.40
      E.8.d.35.80
      E.8.b.30.35

Each Platoon with two Sections on
Forward Bank & two Sections on the
Rear Bank.

O.C "B" will be prepared to exploit
their success up to Junction of HOBART
St with the CANAL-du-NORD LINE.
at E.9.c.05.85. & will co-operate with
Coys on flanks.

4. "A" Coy will be in Support & may
be called by O.C. Forward Coys for
support or carrying.

O.C "A" will be immediately report
to Battn the strength & nature of
support required.

"D" Coy will be in Reserve.

5 (a) Artillery barrage will come down on
the present S.O.S lines at Zero &
will remain there on this line until
Zero plus 4 mins. thence moving
forward by bounds of 100 yds every
5 mins up to the CANAL-du-NORD, French
line where it will remain until

- 2 -

withdrew his men slowly to our jumping off
positions and re-organised our defences.
His initiative and cool-headed resource are
deserving of the highest commendation.

Jno FitzGerald Jones

Major,
Commanding, 8th (Irish) Battn. K.L.R.

20.9.18.

COPY No......16...

8th. (IRISH) BATTN. "THE KING'S" (LIVERPOOL REGT.)

OPERATION ORDER No. 51.

o-o-o-o-o-o-o-o-o-o-o-o-o-o-o o-o-o-o-o-o-

Ref. Map. Sheet.   16.9.18.
51..8. 1/40,000.

1. This Battalion will be relieved by the 1/7th. ROYAL
    SCOTS on 16th. Sept. 1918.

2. Relief will probably commence about 3.30. pm.
        "A" Coy. 8th.K.L.R. relieved by No.1 Coy. Royal Scots

        "B" "   "   "   "2" "   "
        "C" "   "   "   "3" "   "
        "D" "   "   "   "4" "   "

3. (a) On relief Companies will move off in the order -
           H.Q. A. B. C-D.
       to Camp at T.30.a   100 yards distance will be
       Maintained between Platoons.
       Route to be notified later.
   (b) Transport less Lewis Gun Limbers and Field Kitchens
       will move under Transport Officer.

4. Advance Parties will proceed as previously detailed.

5. Relief complete will reported to Battn. H.Q. by O.C.
    Coys. in person.

6. Battn. H.Q. will close at present location on relief
    and will re-open at same hour at T.30.a.

7. ACKNOWLEDGE.

                                        Capt. & Adjt.
                                   8th.(Irish) Battn. K.L.Regt

Issued at 11 am.
    Copies to :-

        1. 171st. Infantry Brigade.
        2. Commanding Officer.
        3. 2nd-in-Command.
        4. Adjutant.
        5/9. Companies.
        10. Transport Officer.
        11. Quartermaster.
        12. Medical Officer.
        13. 1/7th. Royal Scots.
        14. R.S.M.
        15/16 War Diary.
        17. File.
        18. Intelligence Officer.

            o-o-o-o-o-o-o-o-o-o-

ZERO plus 120.

(b) 15 mins after barrage has reached the CANAL-du-NORD, trench line, it will form a box barrage round junction of HOBART ST with CANAL-du-NORD at E.9.c.05.85.
The box will be formed on the trenches at the following points:-
    E.9.a.00.50
    E.9.a.50.25.
    E.9.c.45.45.

6 (a) T.M.B will fire on CEMETERY at E.14.c.70.70.

(b) One detachment will be detailed to move along HOBART ST in rear of parties of 8th K.L.R & will assist in covering consolidation.

7. Flares will be lit by the posts on the CANAL & any posts forward of same at 7 pm.

8. Liaison will be established by O.C. "C" Coy with Right Bn at E.14.b.90.35. & will push a patrol out to CANAL-du-NORD LINE.

— 4 —

9. O.C. Attacking Coys will forward reports on ~~consolidation~~ condition of CANAL as particulars already issued.

10. Battle Aid Post will be at ROWLAND POST.
R.A.P. in present location.

11. Prisoners will be sent to Battn H.Q.

12. Sig. Officer will send watch round for synchronisation at 3pm & 4pm.

13. Reports will be sent to Bn. H.Q. which will remain at present location with Forward Command Post at E.13.b.20.25.

14. Acknowledge.

R N ......
Capt & Adjt
10th M.I.

Copies to:-
1. 171st Infy Bde
2. C.O.
3/6. A.B.C.D Coys
7. S.O
8. M.O.
9/10. War Diary.
11. File.

"JUMI"   Copy No ___
Operation Order No 50 ⑤   14/9/18

1. On the night 12/13th Sept 1918. This Battⁿ will be relieved on the Right Front sector (INCHY) by the 1st Bn. R. MUNSTER Fus.

2. "A" Coy 8th M.S.R will be relieved by "A" R.M.Fs
   B "   "   "   "   "   "   B   "
   C "   "   "   "   "   "   C   "
   D "   "   "   "   "   "   D   "

3. Guides 1 per Platoon + 1 for Bn H.Q will meet incoming Unit at 9.30pm D.6.d.55.05. Each guide will be in possession of a chit shewing the number of his Platoon & the Platoon he is to guide in.

4. All maps, Defence Schemes, Trench Stores & particulars of work in progress & proposed will be carefully handed over & receipts obtained.

5. (a) On relief Coys will move off independently to Billets at V.27.a.6.4 via INCHY - CAGNICOURT Rd to Cross Rds V.28.b.85.90 - Cross Rds V.28.a.40.00 - thence V.27.a.6.4 100 yards distance between Platoons.

- 2 -

5.(c) O.C. Coy will report arrival in person.

6. Advance parties of 1 Officer + 2 N.C.Os. per Coy will proceed from Rear H.Q. to take over billets from R.M.F. at 2pm. They will arrange to meet incoming Coys at V.28.a.40.10 at 12 midnight approx.

7. Relief complete will be reported by wire using code word "PICKETS".

8. Bn H.Q. will close @ present location on relief & re-open at V.27.a.4.4 at same hour.

9. Acknowledge.

R.V. Banbury
Capt & Adjt
7 GWR

Copies to:-
1. 171 Inf Bde
2. B.T.
3/4. 5 Coys
8. I.O.
9. Rear H.Q.
10/11. War Diary
12. File

SECRET.
Copy No. 14.

8th (IRISH) BATTN. "THE KING'S" (LIVERPOOL REGT.)
OPERATION ORDER No. 52.
-o-o-o-o-o-o-o-o-o-o-o-o-o-o-o-o-o-o-

Ref. Map. 51C. 1/40.000.   2459.18.

1. The Battalion (less Transport) will entrain at
   LE HERLIERE on the morning 25th Sept. 1918. moving from
   present location in the order H.Q., A, B, C, D Coys. 100 Yds
   distance between Coys. Via SAULTY. Leading Coy, to pass
   starting Point - Road Junction O.23.d.80.50. at 7a.m.

2. Entraining Officer - 2/Lieut. T.C. McCarthy - will report
   at LE HERLIERE Station at 7a.m. 25th inst.

3. Transport will move by Road Via BARLY - STREINCOURT -
   BIA IREVILLE - BOIS LIEUX au MONT - ST LEGER - CROISILLES
   NOREUIL. Head of column to pass starting point - Cross Roads
   Centre of BARLY at 7a.m.

4. Batt. H.Q. will close at present location at 7a.m. 25.9.18. and
   and will be at head of column en route, reopening on
   arrival at Bivouac Area.

5. A C K N O W L E D G E.

                                        [signature]
                                        Capt & Adjt.,
                                        8th (Irish) Battn. K.L.Regt.

SECRET.   COPY NO. 15

ADMINISTRATIVE INSTRUCTIONS ISSUED IN
ACCORDANCE WITH OPERATION ORDER No. 52.
-o-o-o-o-o-o-o-o-o-o-o-o-o-o-o-o-o-o-o-o-

1. (a) All Mess & Coy. Stores will be dumped at Q.M. Stores to-night.
   (b) Field Kitchens & Lewis Gun Limbers, Maltese Cart, will be ready for Transport Officer at 5.30a.m.
   (c) Officers Valises will be dumped at Q.M. Stores by 5a.m.

2. Unexpended portion of Days Rations will be carried also a few dixes.

3. Dress - Full Marching Order.

4. All Wash Bowls, Meat Safes, and Area Stores will be handed to R.S.M. at once. The R.S.M. will obtain receipts for same from Town Major.

5. Billets will be left in a clean and sanitary condition and a certificate will be obtained and forwarded to J.O.R. by 9a.m. 26.9.18.

6. Reveille. 4.30a.m.   Breakfast 5a.m.

                                        [signature]
                                        Capt. & Adjt.,
                                        8th (Irish) Bttn. K.L.R.

24.9.18.

Secret   8th K.L.R   Copy No. 11
       O.O. 96.

1. This Batt. will be relieved tonight by the 2/4 Loyal N.L.

2. Coys will be relieved as per following
   A Coy 2/4 L.N.L.   A Coy 8 K L R
   B   "   "   B " "
   C   "   "   C " "
   D   "   "   D " "

3. Guides for platoons will meet incoming Unit at 7 p.m. at Cross Tracks (F 7 d 6 2)

4. Coys will move independently to area F 21 b and d.
O.C. Coys will notify relief in person.

5. O.C Coys &c reminded that all petrol tins must be brought out of the line

Acknowledged at 3.45 p.m.
Bde
Coys
10 Qm
PSM

            J.W. Harding
            2/Lt. A/Adj
            8 KLR

SECRET.   COPY NO....
            8th(IRISH) BATTALION "THE KING'S"(LIVERPOOL REGT).
                         OPERATION ORDER NO. 53.
            =o=o=o=o=o=o=o=o=o=o=o=o=o=o=o=o=o=o=o=o=o=o=o=o=o=

Ref: Maps 57c, NE., 1/20,000.
          57b,   1/40,000.   26.9.18.

(1) INFORMATION(1).   On Z day the 57th Division will take part in a
                       general attack.
                            The attack on XVII Corps Front will be
                       made by the 52nd, 63rd, and 57th Divisions.
                            The attack on First(RED Line)objective will
                       be carried out by 52nd and 63rd Divisions. The
                       attack on Second(BROWN Line)objective will be
                       carried out by the 63rd Division, and the 57th
                       Division will then pass through, capturing Third
                       (BLUE Line)objective, and afterwards exploiting
                       success by seizing the crossings over the CANAL
                       DE L'ESCAUT.
                       The CANADIAN CORPS will attack on the Left of
                       57th Division, and the GUARDS Division on the
                       Right.
                       Boundaries and dividing lines between brigades
                       and Battalions are shown on maps already issued

(2) ASSEMBLY,   (2)(a)The Brigade will assemble in the Corps
    APPROACH MARCH   Area West of the Line D.12.a.0.0., D.18.a.0.0.,
    AND DISPOSITIONS   in order from East to West, 2/7th KLR., 1/9th
    OF BRIGADE FOR   KLR.(172 Inf. Bde) 8th K.L.R.(in the Northern
    ATTACK.   Trench of HINDENBURG LINE between Railway at
                       D.15.b.15.85. and hedge at D.16.a.70.45.),
                       2/6th KLR.
                       (b)Assembly will be completed before ZERO. At
                       ZERO the Bde. will close up to the line E.14.a.
                       0.0., E.20.a.0.0., E.26.a.0.0., following the
                       troops of the 63rd Division.
                       (c) Movement to Jumping Off Positions will be
                       made along HINDENBURG front line, through N. side
                       of MOEUVRES, crossing Canal in vicinity of
                       E.15.c.20.30., thence along E.16.c. & d. to
                       BROWN LINE.
                       (d) At ZERO plus 270 minutes(approx)the 171st
                       Inf. Bde. plus 1/9th KLR. will pass through BROWN
                       LINE and will capture and consolidate the
                       CANTAING - FONTAINE NOTRE DAME line (BLUE Line).
                       (e) The Disposition of Battalions will be as under:
                            Right Front Battn: 8th K.L.R.
                            Left   "   "   2/7th KLR.
                            Reserve   "   2/6th K.L.R.

(3) METHOD OF   (3)(a)From the BROWN Line the 2/7th K.L.R. will
    ATTACK.   advance on FONTAINE.
                           (b)2/7th KLR. will be followed by 1/9th KLR.
                       who will clear CANTAING Trench and Support.
                           (c)8th KLR. will follow 1/9th KLR. down
                       CANTAING Support Trench to Inter-Brigade Boundary
                       at SUNKEN ROAD in F.26.b.3.3. when direction will
                       be changed to N.E. and objective advanced upon.
                           (d) 2/6th KLR. will follow 8th KLR. Two
                       Coys. to consolidate and garrison CANTAING SUPPORT
                       and two Coys. to be in readiness to reinforce
                       and support the attack.
                           (e) The attack will be made behind an artillery
                       barrage, details of which will be issued later.

SECRET.

- 2 -

(4) FORMATION & DISTRIBUTION OF BATTALION.

(4)(a) The Battalion will be disposed on a three Company Frontage. The Right and Centre Coys. will attack on a frontage of two platoons - the Left Company on a frontage of one platoon. Reserve Company will move forward on a two Platoon Frontage.

The advance from Jumping Off Point will be made in artillery formation of sectional columns.

(b) Company Boundaries on jumping off line and objective will be as follows:-

Jumping Off Line: Right Front: "A" Coy. Batt. Right Boundary To F.26.b.10.85. both inclus.
Centre Front: "C" Coy. F.26.b.10.85. to F.20.c.80.10. both exclus.
Left Front: "D" Coy. F.20.c.80.10. to Battn. on Left Boundary, both inclusive.
OBJECTIVES. Right Front: "A" Coy. F.23.c.00.80. to F.22.b.90.55. both inclus.
Centre Front: "C" Coy. F.22.b.90.55. to F.15.d.20.20 both exclusive.
Left Front: "D" Coy. F.15.d.20.20. to F.15.Central both inclusive.
Reserve Company: "B" Coy. General area F.21.c. and d.

(c) Immediately after capture, objectives will be consolidated and defence distributed in depth. A series of small tactical posts, particulars of which have been issued separately - which must be mutually supporting, will be made.

(5) COMMUNICATIONS.

(5) See Addendum No.1.

(6) LIAISON.

(6) O.C. Coys. will be responsible for the maintenance of liaison with flank units throughout the advance, and on arrival at the objectives. O.C. "A" Coy. will establish touch with 1st Bn.Royal Munsters at about F.22.d.50.85. and O.C. "B" Coy. at F.21.d.80.30.
O.C. "D" Coy. will establish touch with 2/7th HR. at F.21.b.25.90., F.15.d.70.70., and F.15.c.70.95.

(7) ARTILLERY.

(7) The following is the outline of the Artillery Action. This will be confirmed in Artillery Barrage Table which will be issued later:-
176th Bde.R.F.A. who are attached to the Brigade Group will move over the CANAL at ZERO plus 210 mins. The barrage for 2/7th K.L.R. will lift at ZERO plus 317 mins. off a line running North from F.19.b.70.30. and will move forward at the rate of 100 yards in 5 minutes.

The barrage for the 1/9th KLR. will remain on CANTAING TRENCH for 30 minutes. It will then switch south at the rate of 100 yards in 5 minutes, until it reaches the Sunken Road at the Brigade Boundary F.26.b.2.4. at ZERO plus 390 minutes.

Two 6" T.Ms. are allotted to 171st Inf.Bde. to assist in the operations (details of action will be issued later).

Heavy Artillery will engage targets in the vicinity of FONTAINE NOTRE DAME, and F.21.c. and F.22.d. and c.

-2-

(8) MACHINE GUNS (8) "B" Coy. 57th Bn. M.G.C. will co-operate during the advance and on arrival at objectives; one Section (4 Guns) under 2/Lt. PEARSON will be disposed in the vicinity of F.21.a.4.1.

(9) MEDICAL. (9) The Regimental Aid Post before ZERO will be in vicinity of Battalion HQ. During the advance the Medical Officer will move forward with Battn. HQ. On arrival at objectives Aid Post will be established in CANTAING SUPPORT at approx. F.20.d.00.00.

(10) SYNCHRONISATION OF WATCHES. (10) Watches will be synchronised at 9 p.m. daily until further notice. O.C. Coys. will send two watches to Battn. HQ. for synchronisation at that hour.

(11) ZERO HOUR (11) will be notified later.

(12) BATTN. HQRS. (12) Battalion HQrs. will move forward by bounds in accordance with the various phases of the battle. During assembly it will be at approx. D.15.b.50.70. During approach march it will move to M.23.c.10.55. and from thence to CANTAING SUPPORT at F.20.c.50.30.
2/Lt. F. BURNS with a forward party will proceed to these locations in advance of Battn. HQ. in order to report on the situation and establish Forward Headquarters.
After objectives have been reached a forward report centre will be established at F.21.c.30.70.

(13) REPORTS (13) To BATTALION HEADQUARTERS, through Forward Report Centre.

Attention is directed to the following instructions which have been already issued:-
General Instructions No. 1.
Administrative " No. 1.
Addendum No. 1. - Communications.

Issued at 5 p.m.
TO:- 1.171st Inf. Bde.
2. 2/5th K.L.R.
3. 2/7th K.L.R.
4. 1st Bn. Royal Munster Fus.
5. C.O.
6. Adjutant.
7/11. 5 Coys.
12. Sigs. Off.
13. Intell. Off.
14. T.O.
15. Q.M.
16. R.S.M.
17. M.O.
18.
19. File.
20. War Diary.

Geo. Stickling
Capt. & Adjt. 2nd/8
8th (Irish) Bn. K.L.R.

SECRET.   COPY NO...
              8th (IRISH) BATT. "THE KING'S (LIVERPOOL REGIMENT).
                      ADDENDUM NO. 1. - COMMUNICATIONS.
           -o-o-o-o-o-o-o-o-o-o-o-o-o-o-o-o-o-o-o-o-o-o-ooo---o-

                                                          25.9.18.

(1) Communication during the advance will be maintained
    by Runner, Visual and Pigeons (if available), and later
    when the position is stabilised by Telephone and
    Fullerphone.

(2) Brigade will establish forward report centres as
    follows:-
    (a) Before approach march : N.14.d.20.15.
    (b) During approach march : N.23.c.20.85 (when it will
         connect by lateral lines to An.HQ at
         N.23.c.10.55).
    (c) When Battns. have moved forward to final positions
         in vicinity of N.19.c.9.1. (will lay line to
         Battn. HQ).
    A Trench Wireless set will be established at N.26.d.1.9.
    and will be available for messages to Bde. HQ from this
    Unit.

(3) Visual Communication will be established wherever
    possible at all stages of the operation unless
    distances are close enough to make runners more
    expeditious.

(3) When objectives have been reached all messages will
    be passed to Battn. HQrs. through Forward Report Centre
    at N.21.c.30.70.

(4) All important messages will be sent in duplicate by
    two different routes or means of transmission; those
    of special importance by three different routes or means
    of transmission.   Runners will carry all messages
    in the right hand breast pocket in which nothing else
    will be carried.

(5) CONTACT AND PATROL AEROPLANES. (a) A Contact Aeroplane
    will call for flares on the Third Objective at ZERO
    plus 6 hours and 30 minutes.   Junior Officers as
    well as other ranks will carry flares, and possess the
    means of lighting them.
            It must be continually impressed on all ranks
    that flares <u>must</u> be lighted when called for by the
    Aeroplane.
    (b) A low flying Counter-Attack patrol will be up
    throughout the day from ZERO plus 2 hours onwards.
    The role will be to give notice of a counter-attack
    or to inform the artillery of fleeting targets as they
    appear.
    Should the patrol observe enemy troops moving up within
    1,000 yards of our Infantry, apparently about to
    Counter-attack, it will notify the fact to the Infantry
    by lighting magnesium-wing-tip flares and by dropping
    a <u>RED smoke bomb</u> in the area where the enemy is seen
    assembling or attacking.

    POPHAM PANELS will be kept in readiness.

Issued at 5 p.m.
Copies to:-
  1. C.O.
  2. 2nd in Command.
  3/7. 5 Coys.
  8. Sigs. Off.
  9. 171st Inf. Bde.
 10. File.
 11. War Diary.

                                         for Capt. & Adjt.
                                         8th (Irish) Bn. K.L.R.

           -o-o-o-o-o-o-o-o-o-o-o-o-o-o-

REPORT ON OPERATION WEST OF CAMBRAI - 27.9.18. to 30.9.18.

-o-o-o-o-o-o-o-o-o-o-o-o-o-o-o-o-

Ref. 57C. N.E. 1/20.000.
"   57B. N.W. 1/20.000.

1. The Battalion moved off from Bivouac Area in D.13.a. (S.W. of QUEANT) at 2a.m. on the morning of 27th Sept. to Assembly Positions in Northern portion of HINDENBURG FRONT LINE in D.15.b. & D.16.a. being in Rear of 9th K.L.R. and in front of 6th K.L.R.

2. At Zero Hour (5.40a.m.) the Battalion moved forward in rear of 9th K.L.R. and passing over the CANAL-DU-NORD at MOUVRES followed in wake of the attack which was being carried on by 63rd Division - using the Road which marked the Northern Boundary of the XVII Corps - E.15.c. & d.- E.16.c. & d. - E.17.c. & d.

3. On arrival at approx. E.16.d. the advance of the Battalion was checked. The Commanding Officer (Major J.F. Jones., MC) went forward to reconnoitre and discovered that the 63rd Division had been held up ridge running S.W. in E.23.a. & c. - E.28.d. - E.28.b. by heavy Machine Gun fire from the FACTORY at E.29.a. and Artillery and Machine Gun fire from ANNEUX.

4. This information was passed on to O.C. 6th K.L.R. who was proceeding immediately in rear, and to Headquarters. 171st Infantry Brigade and close liaison was established with Battn. H.Q. of 2nd ROYAL IRISH RIFLES and 7th Battn. ROYAL FUSILIERS in THREX STREET - this Battalion having taken cover behind the Ridge and Battn. H.Q. established at E.16.c.5.4.

5. At about 3.30p.m. it was reported that the FACTORY and ANNEUX had been captured. Brigadier-General F.C. LONGBOURNE., D.S.O., came up at this junction and ordered that at 6.30p.m. the 6th K.L.R. and 8th K.L.R. would pass through the 63rd Division and take original objectives on the BLUE LINE - the 7th K.L.R. having become disorganised owing to heavy Machine Gun fire which inflicted considerable casualties upon them.

6. The Battalion (less "A" Company) which had become attached to 9th K.L.R. in an attack upon ANNEUX earlier in the day, was then moved to Road running through E.22.b. & d. -E.23.c. & E.29.a. and Battn. H.Q. established at E.23.c.10.55.

7. At 6p.m. "B" Company (Capt. E.H. Bennett)- "C" Company (Lieut. F.W. Hogg) and "D" Company (2/Lieut. F.L.Elsworth) moved off from this position for their objectives. When they arrived about 800 yards from ANNEUX the S.O.S. signal was put up in many places and troops of another Division and another Brigade fell back in disorder upon our advancing columns. Our men pressed on and found a Counter-Attack in progress which they assisted to repel. Our protective barrage continued to fall immediately in of ANNEUX and it was impossible to proceed. The three Companies were therefore withdrawn to positions in Area E.30.b. with a view to resuming the advance when the situation permitted. Whilst in this position they were ordered by O.C. 2/5th K.O.R. to consider themselves under the his command and that they would be employed in the defence of the village. On learning of this Company Commanders were at once instructed that they were not under the command of this Officer and that whilst they must maintain close liaison with him they were to hold their Companies ready for Offensive action.

8. At this time (7.30p.m.) the situation appeared to be that

-2-

the Eastern Edge of GRAINCOURT was being held by the 1st
ROYAL MUNSTER FUSILIERS and elements of the 63rd Division
- the line then running back to SUNKEN ROAD in E.30.c. & d.
which was held by 2/5th K.O.R.I. and from thence along S.E.
Edge of ANNEUX to BROWN LINE in E.28.a. which was held by
ROYAL MARINE LIGHT INFANTRY.

9½. At 12.30a.m. 28.9.18. the Brigade Major called at Battn. H.Q.
and said that orders were on the way for the attack to be
resumed in co-operation with 172nd Infantry Brigade at 6.30am.
that morning. The plan was that a bombardment was to be put
down on the Divisional Area at 5.15a.m. and at 6.30a.m. the
171st & 172nd Infantry Brigades were to advance and capture
the BLUE LINE. The 6th K.L.R. were to move on North side
of CAMBRAI - BAUPAUME Road and clear up situation South of
FONTAINE afterwards working down SUNKEN ROAD in F.21.b. & d.
to gain touch with 172nd Infantry Brigade. 7th K.L.R. were
to work down MARQUION LINE and 2 Companies of this Battalion
were to follow in close support to 6th K.L.R. pass through
them and clear up FONTAINE - afterwards establishing Posts
EAST of FONTAINE.

10. "B" & "D" Companies were at once ordered to move to SUNKEN RD
at E.24.b. for purpose of establishing touch with 6th K.L.R.
At 6a.m., as neither 6th or 7th K.L.R. had arrived at this
point these 2 Companies commenced the advance and moving
quickly forward they found that FONTAINE had been cleared by
CANADIANS - established Posts as ordered and sent Patrols
Southwards to establish touch with 172nd Infy. Bde. They
were joined about 3/4Hr later by 6th & 7th K.L.R. whose
orders for the operations had been delayed.

11. On completion of this operation the 6th & 7th K.L.R. were
ordered to take over the line and this Battalion was withdrawn
to SUPPORT in SUNKEN ROAD in F.21.c. (B & D Coys.) and
MARQUION LINE F.20.c. (A & C Coys. & Battn. H.Q.)

12. At 11a.m. 29.9.18. instructions were received that the Battn.
would take the MARCOING LINE between the CAMBRAI - BAUPAUME
ROAD in F.17.a. & b. and the CANAL in F.23.b. & F.24.a.
"B" & "C" Companies were ordered to assemble in SUNKEN ROAD
in F.22.b. & d. with One Section L.T.M. and "D" Company was
ordered to assemble astride the Light Railway in SUNKEN ROAD
in F.16.a.
The plan of the operation was that "D" Company would advance
to the Northern Edge of the Line taking advantage of the
Railway Embankment and would work down the MARCOING Line and
support with two Platoons in each. "B" & "C" Companies were
to work Northwards from the Lock House in F.24.a. - "B" Coy. up
the MARCOING SUPPORT and "C" Company up the MARCOING LINE.
the enterprise being assisted by Light Trench Mortar fire
from the SUNKEN ROAD in F.17.d. if necessary. Just as this
operation was on the point of commencing it was cancelled by
telephonic order from the Brigade and an order to assemble in
the Area F.23.a. was received. This was done by 5p.m.

13. Orders were then received that 6th K.L.R. would seize the
crossings over the CANAL-DE-ST QUENTIN at F.24.a.3.9. and
A.13.c.3.2. - that 7th K.L.R. were to cross and move on
PROVILLE and 8th K.L.R. was to hold itself in readiness to
cross the CANAL. O.C.6th K.L.R. asked that his left flank
should be secured and in order to do this "C" Company were
ordered to occupy the MARCOING LINE in F.17.d. & F.18.c.
The orders were varied later - 6th K.L.R? effecting a crossing
and moving on PROVILLE - 7th K.L.R. moved to a position in
SUPPORT along Northern Bank of CANAL in LA FOLIE WOOD and
8th K.L.R. remained in Area F.22.c. with "C" Company in
MARCOING LINE.

14. At 12.30a.m. orders were received that this Battalion would

establish a line from A.13.d.0.0. to A.8.d.0.9. with responsibility for clearing up situation in Railway Triangle in A.9.a. This operation was concluded by 6a.m. with two Platoons E. of the RIVER - keeping in touch with 6th K.L.R. on Right and CANADIAN MOUNTED RIFLES on left. One wounded prisoner was taken during the night and was evacuated to Field Ambulance. It was found necessary to withdraw the advanced Posts which had been established at Railway Triangle in A.9.a. as this Area was being heavily shelled by our own as well as enemy guns. Battn. H.Q. were established at F.23.b.90.60.

15. O.C. 7th K.L.R. having sent the information that he was to attack PROVILLE at 1.20p.m., orders were issued to O.C. "D" Company to assist this movement by Lewis Gun & Rifle fire. from Railway Embankment and A.14.c. and a Section of L.T.Ms. were detailed to co-operate from S.E. Corner of WOOD in A.13.d. The Operation on PROVILLE having been successful and O.C. 7th K.L.R. having stated that he was unable the Area between the CANL-DE-ST QUENTIN and the ESCAUT RIVER - two Platoons were pushed forward into A.14.c. for this purpose. "B" Company on Left and "A" Company on Right were ordered to conform to the advance and the general line - A.14.c.40.00. - A.14.c.90.70. - A.3.d.10.90. - 3 was taken up. "C" Company were ordered to take up positions in close support A.13.b. & d. and "A" Company were ordered into Reserve in MARCOING LINE in F.18.c.

16. The Battalion was relieved at 10p.m. by 2/4th Bn. L.N.L.R.

17. Casualties during the foregoing operation were as follows:-

    OFFICERS:-   Killed.   2/Lieut. H.H. Shepherd.

                 Wounded.   Capt. W.T. Ball., M.C.
                              2/Lieut. G. Grant.
                              " R.L. Smither.

    OTHER RANKS.   Killed.   Eight. (8)
                         Missing.   Six. (6)
                         Wounded. Forty-nine. (49)

Major,
Commanding, 8th (Irish) Battn. K. L. Regt.

3.10.18.

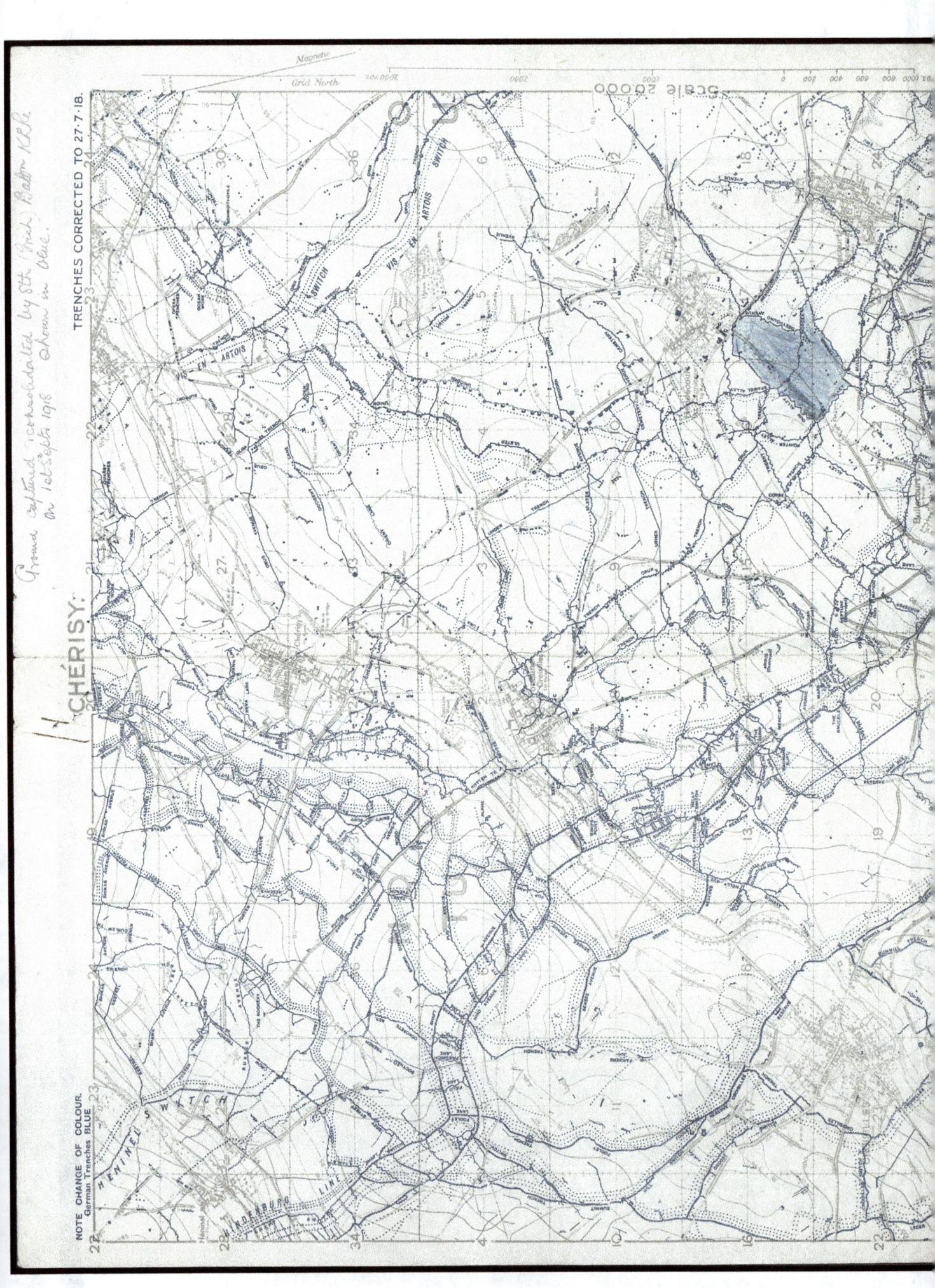

Reference Sketch on back.

To

1. My {Platoon / Company} has reached

   (Mark position on map or give map reference).

   and is consolidating.
   has consolidated.
   is ready to advance.

2. I am (not) in touch with   on right

   and (not) with   on left.

3. I am held up at   {by wire.
                                             by M.G. fire.
                                             by rifle fire.

4. Enemy's artillery is firing on

              from

5. I have sent forward patrols to

6. I estimate {my casualties at
               my strength at

7. I need   boxes S.A.A.
               Lewis gun drums
               Bombs
               Rifle Grenades
               Stokes Shells
               Very Lights   (at once)
               Ground Flares   (to-night)
               Stakes
               Coils wire
               Tins water
               Rations

8. I intend to

9. (General remarks on position and strength of enemy. Number of prisoners taken and identifications, if known).

Time   Name   Rank
Date   Platoon   Coy
                Battalion

Strike out all that is not applicable and forward at once to Bn. H.Q.

REFERENCE SKETCH ON BACK

To ....

1. MY { PLATOON } HAS REACHED ....
      { COMPANY }
                                    (MARK POSITION ON MAP OR GIVE
                                     MAP REFERENCE).

   AND IS CONSOLIDATING ....
       HAS CONSOLIDATED ....
       IS READY TO ADVANCE ....

2. I AM (NOT) IN TOUCH WITH .... ON RIGHT.
        AND (NOT) WITH .... ON LEFT.

3. I AM HELD UP AT ....   BY WIRE.
                                         BY M.G. FIRE.
                                         BY RIFLE FIRE.

4. ENEMY'S ARTILLERY IS FIRING ON ....
                           FROM ....

5. I HAVE SENT FORWARD PATROLS TO ....

6. I ESTIMATE { MY CASUALTIES AT ....
              { MY STRENGTH AT ....

7. I NEED   BOXES S.A.A.
             LEWIS GUN DRUMS.
             BOMBS.
             RIFLE GRENADES.
             STOKES SHELLS.   (AT ONCE)
             VERY LIGHTS.
             GROUND FLARES.   (TO-NIGHT)
             STAKES.
             COILS WIRE.
             TINS WATER.
             RATIONS.

8. I INTEND TO ....

9. (GENERAL REMARKS ON POSITION AND STRENGTH OF ENEMY. NUMBER
    OF PRISONERS TAKEN AND IDENTIFICATIONS, IF KNOWN).

TIME .... NAME .... RANK ....
DATE .... PLATOON .... COY. ....
                BATTALION ....

STRIKE OUT ALL THAT IS NOT APPLICABLE AND FORWARD AT ONCE TO BN. H.Q.

8th (Irish) Batt. "The Kings" (Liverpool) Regiment

WAR DIARY

Army Form C. 2118.

INTELLIGENCE SUMMARY.
(Erase heading not required.)

SECRET

October 1918.

Place	Date	Hour	Summary of Events and Information	Remarks and references to Appendices
PROVILLE Sheet 57B N.W.A.20.b.	October 1st 1918.		Strength. Effective 39. Off. 690 O.R. Ration 24 Off. 500. O.R. A full report of operations west of CAMBRAI from the 1st – 9th October 1918 is attached. Casualties for that period 1. Officer killed (2nd Lt. J. Quinn). 4. O.R. killed. 1. Officer died of wounds (2nd Lt. T. Spenalow). 1. Officer wounded (2nd Lt. R.H. Hunt). 18. O.R. wounded.	①
	October 10th. 1918.		Moved from PROVILLE by march route to bivouac area near BOURSIES. Sheet 57.N.E. D.24.d. remaining there two days.	
BOURSIES	October 12th 1918.		Moved by march route to Siding near HERMIES. Sheet 57C N.E. J.34.a. Entraining there at 1400 hours (12th) and detraining at 05.00 hours on the 13th at FOUQUEREUIL moving by march route to billets at HAILLICOURT Ref. Sheet 44 B. T.18.a.	②
HAILLICOURT	October 14th. 1918		Re-organization of the Battalion. Cleaning up & smartening up drill. Carried out.	
	October 15th. 1918.		Moved from HAILLICOURT by Bus. Original orders for this move were to relieve a Batt. of the 173rd Inf. Bde. In a reserve position to the 47th Div. at BAS MAISNIL. These were altered on debussing at PONT-DE-HEM. Ref. Sheet HAZEBROUCK 5a. 5. J.04.20. from where the Battn. moved to billets at LAVENTIE Ref Sheet HAZEBROUCK 5a. 5. J. 25. 53.	③

Commandg. 8th (Irish) Batt. "The Kings" (Liverpool) Regt.

8th (Service) Battn. The King's (Liverpool) Regiment.

WAR DIARY
INTELLIGENCE SUMMARY.

(Erase heading not required.)

SECRET

October 1918.

Army Form C. 2118.

Place	Date	Hour	Summary of Events and Information	Remarks and references to Appendices
	October 16th. 1918.		The move by march route to BAS MAISNIL was resumed but again orders were altered En route and the Battn. relieved the 2/4th Battn. South Lancs Regt. in reserve position at FROMELLES Ref. Sheet. 36. N.23. a. 30.20. The Brigade was in Reserve. Reconnaissance of forward area by Officers.	(4)
	October 17th-23rd		A full report on operations carried out between these dates is attached.	(5)
HONNEVAIN	October 24th.		Brigade relief - This Battn. relieved in support by the 2/4th Battn. South Lancs Regt. and withdrew to billets at RUE FRANCHE Ref Sheet. 37. M.11.	(6)
RUE FRANCHE	October 25th-28th		Re-organization of the Battn. Specialist & Company training.	
	October 29th		Inspection of the Battn. by Brig. Genl. G. Meynell. C.M.G. Commdg 171st Infy Bde.	
	October 30th.		Commencement of Divisional Relief. 141 Infy Bde relieving 171 Infy Bde. This Battn. relieved by the 18th Battn. London Regt. (The London Irish) and moved by march route to billets in HELLEMMES Sheet 36. Q.12. a. q. t.	(7)
	October 31st		Specialist & Company Training. Strength. Effective 37. Off. 7703. ORs. Ration 25. Off. 9.586. ORs.	

E. Joyce Major

Commdg. 8th (Service) Battn. The King's (Liverpool) Regt.

Report on Operations carried out from
1st to 9th October.
1918.
-o-o-o-o-o-o-o-o-o-o-o-o-o-o-o-

Ref. Map Sheets:-
57C. N.E.
57B. N.W.

From the 1st to 3rd October the 171st Infantry Brigade was in Divisional Reserve. This Battalion was bivouaced in Area - F.21.b. with Battn. H.Q. at F.21.b.40.30.
During this period the Battalion was reorganized and cleaned up.
Nature of Training :-
Squad & Arms Drill & Platoon Formations.
Cutting out of M.Gs.

On the night of 4th/5th October the Battalion took over the Front Line on Left Sector of the Brigade Front - as per sketch map attached. Shown in blue.
Battn. H.Q. at F.23.b.9.7.
Posts North of the CANAL DE ST QUENTIN were taken over from the 2/4th L.N.L.Regt, and those South of the Canal from the 2/5th K.O.R.L. Regt.
2/7th K.L.Regt. held Posts on the Right and the Canadian Corps held the Posts on the Left.

On the night 6th/7th October the Battalion was relieved by the 2/6th (Rifle) Battn. K.L.Regt, and withdrew into Support positions (as per attached sketch map). shown in red.
Battn. H.Q. at F.23.a.0.4.
This tour in the line was quiet, enemy activity consisting chiefly of T.M. fire.

On the night of 8th/9th October. the Battalion took over the Posts in PROVILLE from the 2/7th K.L.Regt. (as per attached sketch map). Battn. H.Q. at F.24.a.1.5. shown in brown.
The 2/6th (Rifle) Battn. K.L.R. holding Posts on the Left and 1st Bn. Royal Munster Fus. holding Posts on the Right.
At this stage it was reported that the enemy was likely to retire from CAMBRAI during the night. Patrols were pushed forward from all Posts to reconnoitre known enemy positions. Touch was gained with the enemy each time up to 0330 Hours on the 9th October. As a result of one encounter 2/Lieut. F. Openshaw was wounded (afterwards died of wounds) by M.G. fire at close range. Two Patrols which went out at 0430 Hours on 9th October reported that the enemy had vacated his Posts and that they were pushing on.

At 0815 Hours on 9th October. orders were received for the Battalion to move forward in conjunction with troops on flanks.
At 1000 Hours the Battalion moved forward.
"A" Coy. (Right Front) along Road past Fbg.St SEPULCRE, N.E. from A.20.b.
"B" Coy. (Left Front) along Road past FACTORY, N.E. from A.20.b.
"C" Coy. in Support to trench in A.15.c. & A.21.b.
"D" Coy. in Reserve to N.E. outskirts of PROVILLE.

"A" & "B" Coys. had orders to mop up ground on both flanks and meet on ARRAS - CAMBRAI Road in A.16.a.
This objective was reached without opposition and at 1130 Hours, on orders from Brigade "A" & "B" Coys. were withdrawn to positions in A.15. Central.
Battn. H.Q. were established at A.20.b.20.15.
At 1600 Hours on 9th October, the Battalion concentrated in the Village of PROVILLE. Battn. H.Q. at A.20.b.20.15.

Major
Commdg. 8th (Irish) Battn.
The Kings' (Liverpool) Regiment

-o-o-o-o-o-o-o-o-o-

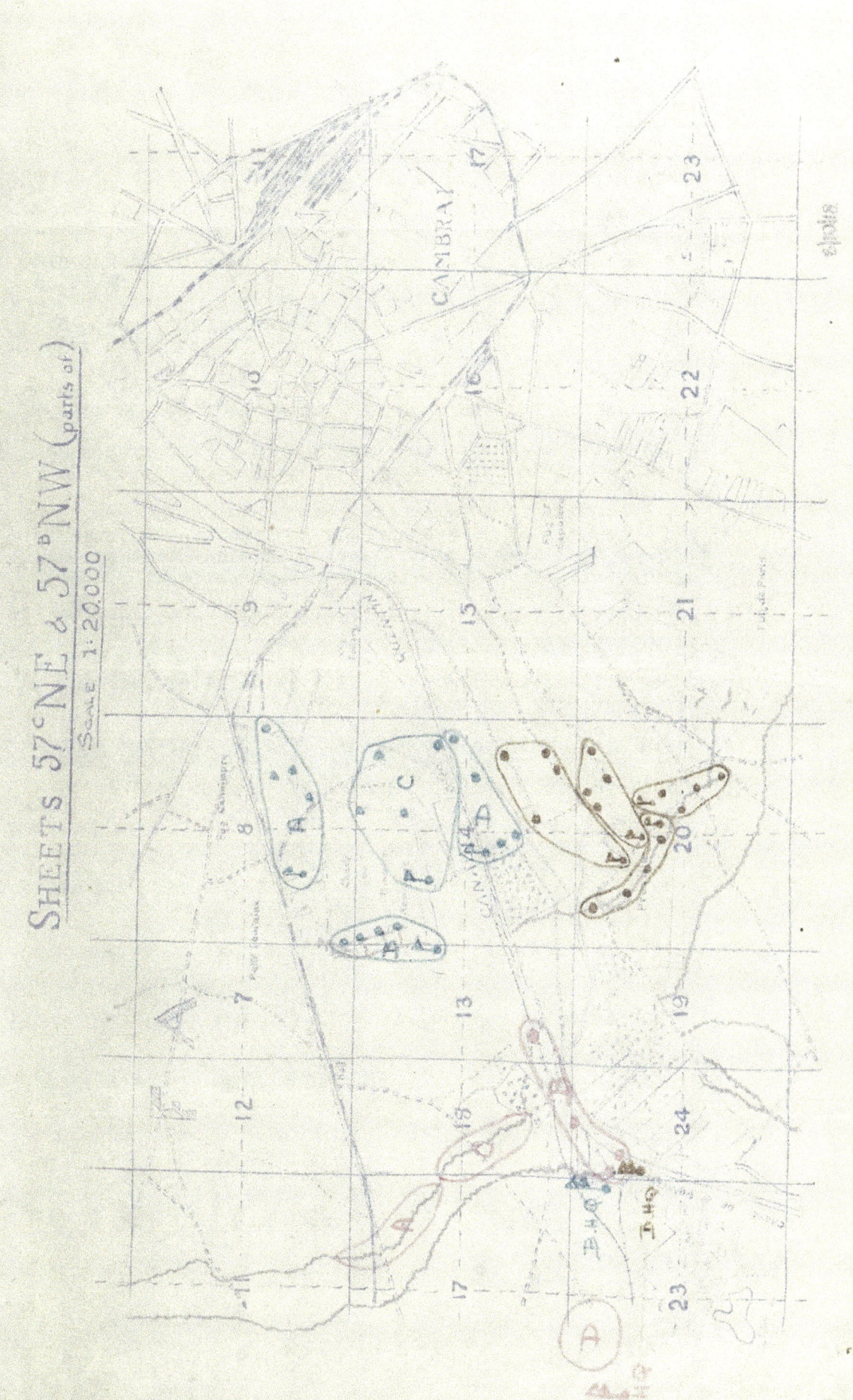

SECRET.
8th (IRISH) BATTN. "THE KING'S" (LIVERPOOL REGIMENT).

COPY NO. 18

OPERATION ORDER No. 56.
-o-o-o-o-o-o-o-o-o-o-o-o-o-o-o-o-o-o-o-o-o-

Ref: Map 57c, NE., 1/20,000.
57h, NW., 1/20,000.

4.10.18.

(1) This Battalion will relieve the 2/4th L.N.Lan.R. and 2/5th K.O.R.Lan.R. on night 4/5th October 1918.

(2) Coys. will take over as follows:-

"A" Coy. 8th KLR. take over from "B" Coy. 2/4th LNLan.R.
"C" " " " " " "C" " and one platoon
                                            "D" Coy. 2/4th L.N.Lan.R.
"B" " " " " " Coy. HQrs. of "B", "C", and
                                            "D" Coys. 2/4th L.N.Lan.R.
"D" " " " " " from "B" & "C" Coys. 2/5th
                                            K.O.R.Lan.R.

Dispositions will be as marked on maps of Coy. Cdrs.

(3) Guides will meet "A", "B", and "C" Coys. at 1900 hours at F.17.d.95.60. and "D" Coy. at F.23.b.95.70. (Bn. HQ) at 1900.hours.

(4) 2/Lt. H. Boothman and 6 Runners will establish a Forward Command Post at "B" Coy. HQrs. The Signalling Officer will lay a line to this point tonight.

(5) Regimental Aid Post will be established in vicinity of Battn. HQrs.

(6) Coys. will send two watches to Signalling Officer at 1800 hours for synchronisation.

(7) Battn. HQrs. will be established at F.23.b.95.70.

(8) Reports : To Battn. HQ. through Forward Command Post.
Relief Complete will be notified by code word "RECEIVED".
ACKNOWLEDGE.

Issued at 1750 hours.
TO: 1. 171 Inf. Bde.
2. 2/4th LNLan.R.
3. 2/5th K.O.R.Lan.R.
4. C.O.
5. 2nd in Cd.
6. Adjutant.
7/11. 5 Coys.
12. Intell. Off.
13. M.O.
14. T.O. & Q.M.
15. RSM.
16. File.
17. War Diary.

A.W. Hickling
2/Lieut. & A/Adjt.
8th(Irish)Batt.K.L.R.

SECRET. COPY No...

8th (IRISH) BATTN. "THE KING'S" (LIVERPOOL REGT.)

Administrative Instructions with
reference to Operation Order No. 56.
-o-o-o-o-o-o-o-o-o-o-o-o-o-o-o-o-o-o-o-o-o-o-

4.10.18.

1. <u>Dress & Equipment</u>. As laid down for last operation, plus Leather Jerkin.

2. <u>Kits</u>. Officers' Valises will be dumped by "D" Coy. H.Q. at 1800 hours. Men's surplus kits will be dumped by "D" Coy. H.Q. at 1600 hours. These must be in sandbags.

3. <u>Ammunition</u>. 5000 Rounds. 40 Magazines (filled) will be dumped with rations at Battn. H.Q. F.24.a.4.7.

4. <u>Rations & Water</u>. Rations & Water for HQrs. will be dumped at Batt. H.Q. F.24.a.4.7. Rations & Water for A.B.C.D. Coys. will be dumped at Cross Tracks F.17.d.6.2. Coys. will arrange for guides to be at these points until parties draw rations.

5. Field Kitchens will be ready to move at 1800 Hours.

2/Lieut. & A/Adjt.
T.D.O.

Issued at 3p.m.
To all recipients of O.O.56.

Secret.   8th KLR OO 58.   War diary
                             Copy No.
                             8.10.18

Ref: 59c NE
     59 F. NW

① This Bn. will relieve 2/7 KLR in the
line on afternoon of 8.10.18.
② Coys. will take over as follows:
A Coy 8th KLR (Right front) from B Coy 2/7 KLR
B   "   "   Centre   D
C   "   "   Left   C
D   "   "   Reserve   A
③ Platoon guides of 2/7 KLR for A, C, and
D Coys will meet Coys at Lock House
at 15.45 hours.
Guides for B Coy at F 24 b. 6. 50.
at 15.45 hours.
④ Advance parties of 1 NCO per platoon
and 1 NCO and 3 OR. for Coy HQ and
1 NCO for Bn. HQ will proceed to
2/7 KLR to take over.
⑤ Lt. Reading with 6 Runners from
Bn. HQ and 2 from each Coy will
establish Forward Command Post at A. 20. b. 20. 15.

(6) Bn HQ will be established at F.24 b 10.50.
(7) Regtl Aid Post will be at A.20 b 15.25
(8) Reports: to Bn HQ through forward Command Post.
(9) Relief complete will be notified by Code word "BABY".
(10) Coys will move off in order CABD - 300 X
Acknowledge between pelotons

Ru Hickling
2/Lt A/Adj
TEDO.

Issued at 1230 hours
To: 1. 17½ 2/L Bn
    2. CO
    3ᴬ 2/L Kirk
    8/7 5 Coys
    8. TO ROM
    9/10 2IC Area Diary

Secret.   7th Do. O.O. No 52   Copy No 11

① The Bn will be relieved by 2/6th L.L.R.
 on night of 6/7th Oct. 1918.
② Coys will be relieved as follows:-
 A Coy 8th K.L.R. by B Coy 2/6th K.L.R.
 B   "   "   C   "   "
 C   "   "   A   "   "
 D   "   "   D   "   "
③ A and C Coys will detail guides
 for posts to meet B and A Coys of
 2/6th K.L.R. at their respective H.Q.s
 on the MARCOING LINE at 18.45 hours.
 B Coy will detail guides for posts
 to meet C Coy of 2/6th K.L.R. where
 Sunken Road cuts the MARCOING LINE.
 D Coy will detail guides for posts
 to meet D Coy 2/6 K.L.R. at Lock
 area at 18.45 hours.
④ After relief this Bn will move
 into MARCOING Support. A and C
 Coys will take over MARCOING LINE—
 Left and Right respectively. B Coy
 will take over the defence of the Canal

- Bridges as detailed in L.48.
- D Coy will move to fields adjacent
- to Lodge Gate at F.22. f 95.40.
(5) Guides for B Coy will be at Lock
House at 19.00 hours.
Guides will not be supplied for
A C and D Coys
(6) After relief. Bn HQ will be established
at F.22. f 95.40.
(7) Relief complete will be notified by
Code word "DOG."

Acknowledge.

Issued at 15:45 hours
To: 1. 17 Bde
    2. CO
    3/4. Coys
    8. Mortars
    9. TO & QM
    10. IO
    11-12. War Diary A/c

[signature]
Lt. A/Adjt
TEDO

Secret.   C.13

                    TEDO Operation Order

(1) <u>Information</u>.   Our troops are reported in
    CAUROIR   B.9.d. and B.10.c. and in
    AWOINGT   B.26.a.

(2) <u>Operations</u>.   172 Bde. are pushing forward
    2 Coys. up road from Fbg de PARIS to
    Railway at A.16 central.
    2/6 K.L.R. are pushing forward 2 Coys. along
    Railway running S.E. from A.9.a. to
    A.16 central and one Coy. along CANAL
    BANK.

(3) A Coy 8 K.L.R. will push forward along
    road from A.20.b. N.E. through
    FBG St SEPOLCRE to Railway.
    B Coy 8 K.L.R. will push forward along
    road from A.20.b. past factory
    to railway.
         Mopping up all ground on
    either side of these roads
    C Coy 8 K.L.R. will move up in support
    and takes up position in trench
    A.15.c. and B.21.b.

- D. Coy 8 KLR. will move on the NE Edge of PROUILLE in reserve.

(4) Indn. Bgn. HQ. will be at present report centre – PROUILLE (A.20.f.20.15)

(5) Coys. will maintain touch laterally and in depth by connecting files during the advance.

(6) Movement forward will commence at 10.00 hours.

2/Lt Cheshire
for A/Adjt Yeo

Ords.
9:10

SECRET.   COPY NO...
    8th (IRISH) BATT. "THE KING'S" (LIVERPOOL REGIMENT).
                    OPERATION ORDER NO. 59.
    -o-o-o-o-o-o-o-o-o-o-o-o-o-o-o-o-o-o-o-o-o-o-

Ref: Map VALENCIENNES., 1/100,000.
                                                              11.10.18.

(1) The Battalion, less "C" Coy. will entrain at
    HERMIES to-morrow for new area.

(2) The Battalion, less "C" Coy. will parade at
    09.45 hours and move off at 10.00 hours, in
    following order, HQrs, A, B, and D Coys. 100 yds.
    distance between Companies.

(3) DRESS: Full Marching Order; Jerkins and Soft
    Caps will be worn. Shrapnel Helmets strapped
    on packs.

(4) "C" Coy. and Transport will move off at 08.15 hours
    and arrive at PREMICOURT STATION at 10.50 hours.
    The following Officer will also move with Transport
                    Capt. H.G. CLARKE.
    Following will compose the Transport:-

	Off.	OR.	Horses.	4 W.V.	2 W.V.
2 Cookers.	1.	-	-	-	-
1 Water Cart.		4.	4.	2.	-
1 Baggage Wagon.		1.	2.	-	1.
1 Mess Cart.		2.	2.	1.	-
4 Riding Horses.		1.	1.	-	1.
L.G.s.		4.	4.	-	-
		1.	2.	1.	-
"C" Company.	4.	100.			

(5) Unloading Party. "C" Coy. will act as unloading party
    on detachment at FOUQUEREUIL.

(6) DISCIPLINE. Picquets will be provided at all stops
    for each end of the train to prevent troops leaving.
    No soldier will detrain without the permission of an
    Officer.

(7) All doors of covered trucks and carriages will be
    kept closed on the right hand side of the train when on
    the main line.
        The brake vans on all types of trains are entirely
    for use of railway staff. No baggage may be loaded
    in them.

ACKNOWLEDGE.

Issued at 13.00 hours.
TO: 1. 171 Inf. Bde.
    2. C.O.
    3. 2nd in Cd.
    4. Adjt.
    5/9. 5 Coys.
    10. I.O.
    11. M.O.
    12. Q.M.
    13. R.S.M.
    14. File.
    15/16. War Diary.

                                    2/Lt. & A/Adjt.
                                    8th (Irish) Batt. K.L.R.

SECRET.   COPY No... 1

8th (IRISH) BATTN. "THE KING'S" (LIVERPOOL REGT.)

OPERATION ORDER No. 60.
-o-o-o-o-o-o-o-o-o-o-o-o-o-o-o-o-o-o-o-

Ref. Map Sheets:-   14.10.18.
  36. 1/40.000.
  LENS II. 1/100.000.
  HAZEBROUCK. 5A. 1/100.000.

1. The Battalion will move to-morrow by Bus and March Route to Billets at BAS MAISNIL (Ref. Hazebrouck.5A. 5.K.62.36.)

2. The Battalion will parade at 0830 Hours on "C" Coys. Parade Ground (Ref. LENS II. I. B.05.70.)
   Dress :- Full Marching Order - Soft Caps - Blankets wrapped in ground sheets strapped together with Steel Helmets on Packs.

3. Embussing Point will be on HAILLICOURT - BARLIN ROADS. Route via BETHUNE - LOCON - VIEILLE CHAPPELLE - PONT DE HEM-PONT LOGY - (Map Ref. Hazebrouck 5A. 5.J.20.04.) where Battalion will debuss and march via Road Junction Sheet 36. M.34.b.3.6. - PIETRE - Road Junction Sheet 36. N.31.d.1.1.- AUBERS and Fromelles to destination.

4. An Officer or Senior N.C.O. will be in charge of each Bus. No man will leave a Bus without the permission of an Officer.

5. Transport will move by Road, passing Cross Roads, HAILLICOURT at 1030 Hours. Route via BETHUNE - RICHEBOURG L'AVOUE - PONT LOGY.

6. On arrival in new Area the Battalion will relieve 1st Battn Royal Munster Fusiliers The Brigade being in the Support Area.

                                    H. Cheshire
ACKNOWLEDGE.

                                    Lieut & A/Adjt.,
                                    8th (Irish) Battn. K.L.Regt.

Issued at 1900 Hours.

  Copies to :-

    1. 171st Infy. Bde.
    2. C.O.
    3. 2nd-in-Cd.
    4. Adjutant.
    5/9. 5 Coys.
    10. Medical Officer.
    11. Quartermaster.
    12. Transport Officer.
    13. Intell. Officer.
    14. R.S.M.
    15/16. War Diary.
    17. File.

-o-o-o-o-

ACHM. COPY No.7...

8th (IRISH) BATTN. "THE KING'S" (LIVERPOOL REGT.)
ADMINISTRATIVE INSTRUCTIONS ISSUED WITH
OPERATION ORDER No. 60.

=-=-=-=-=-=-=-=-=-=-=-=-=-=-=

14.10.19.

1. Officers Valises, Mess Kits, Orderly Room Stores, Coy. Stores Etc., will be dumped at Q.M. Stores by 0800 hours.

2. Cookers and Lewis Gun Limbers will be ready for Transport Officer by 0800 hours.

3. Haversack Rations will be carried. Dinner will be served on arrival at new Area. One Cook per Company will accompany Cookers.

4. Billets will be left in a clean and sanitary condition and will be ready for inspection by the 2nd-in-Command at 0900 hours.

5. One Lorry will be available for transport of stores. Quartermaster will send a guide for same to Bde. H.Q. by 0900 hours.

H. Chestnut
Lieut & A/Adjt.,
8th (Irish) Battn. K.L.Regt.

To all recipients of O.O.60.

UNIT: 8th(IRISH) BATT. THE KING'S (LIVERPOOL REGT).   COPY N°..
               OPERATION ORDER NO.61.
             -o-o-o-o-o-o-o-o-o-o-o-

Ref: Sheet 36, 1/40,000.   15.10.18.

   (1)   The Battalion will move today, 15.10.18. by march
         route to LE MAISNIL (Ref: G.36. c.13.)

   (2)   The Battalion will move off in order Bn. HQrs, A, B, C,
         and D Coys., leading Company to pass starting point
         at present Battn. HQ. at 0915 hours.
         Dress: Full Marching Order - Steel helmets -
         blanket wrapped in ground sheet and strapped on pack -
         jerkins will be worn.

   (3)   Route: VIA HARLECH ROAD - LICANTIS ROAD to ROAD
         JUNCTION N.7.c.95.00. - V.C.CORNER N.7.c.9.1. - RUE
         DELVAS to ROAD JUNCTION N.15.a.85.50. - FROM LIES -
         LE MAISNIL.

   (4)   Location of Unit will be notified on arrival at
         LE MAISNIL.

   (5)   Transport: Only Cookers, S.A.A. Limbers, Water Carts,
         and Mess Cart will accompany Battalion. Remainder
         of transport will remain at LAVENTIE pending further
         instructions.

   (6)   Brigade HQrs. will be at G.13.a.4.8. on arrival.

   (7)   Bde. will be in Divisional Reserve - Battalion will be
         prepared to relieve in line.

   ACKNOWLEDGE.

                                    H. Cheshire
                                    _____
                                    Lieut. & A/Adjt.
Issued at 0930 hours.   8th(Irish) Batt.K.L.R.
TO:-
   1.   171 Inf. Bde.
   2.   C.O.
   3.   2nd in C.
   4.   Adjt.
   5/9. 5 Coys.
   10. I.O.
   11. M.O.
   12. T.O.
   13. S.M.
   14. R.M.
   15. File.
   16. War Diary.

           -o-o-o-o-o-o-o-o-o-o-o-o-

SECRET.   COPY NO..

   8th (IRISH) BATTALION K.L.R.
   Administrative Instructions with
   reference to Operation Order 61.
       -o-o-o-o-o-o-o-o-o--

                                        16.10.18.

   (1) Officers Valises, Mess Kits, and Batt.
       Orderly Room stores will be dumped at
       QM. stores by 0830 hours; 16.10.18.

   (2) Cookers and L.G. Limbers will be ready for
       T.O. by 0830 hours 16.10.18.

   (3) All rations for the day will be carried
       on Cookers.

                                    [signature]

                                    Lieut. & A/Adjt.
Issued at 0100 hours.   8th (Irish) Batt. K.L.R.
To all recipients of
  O.O.61. (less Bde).

       -o-o-o-o-o-o-o-

SECRET.   COPY NO...67

                8th (IRISH) BATTN. "THE KING'S" (LIVERPOOL REGT.)
                          OPERATION ORDER No. 62.
                    -o-o-o-o-o-o-o-o-o-o-o-o-o-o-o-o-

Ref. Map Sheet.   16.10.18.
36. 1/40.000.

1. The 171st Infantry Brigade will pass through the Left
   Battalion of the 142nd Infantry Brigade and continue the
   advance in a N.E. direction at 0930 hours to-morrow,
   17th inst.

2. 2/6th (Rifle) Battn. K.L.Regt. will be Right Front Battn.
   2/7th Battn. K.L.Regt.   "   " Left   "   "
   8th (Irish) Battn. K.L.Regt.   "   " in Support.

3. This Battalion will take up positions as under:-

   "C" Coy. Right Front. Vicinity N.E. End of BIE de la GUERRE.)
   "D" "   Left Front.   "   O.11.b.   (O.11.d. & O.17.b)
   "B" Coy. Support. Vicinity - Eastern End EL CORCQUES -)
                                                 O.11.c.)
   "A" "   Reserve.   "   - Railway O.16.a.

   Battn. H.Q. will at first be established at O.17.c.3.7.
   Brigade H.Q. will at first be established at CHATEAU de
                                        FLANDRES (O.16.d.2.5.)

4. The Battalion will move from present location in the order
   "D" - "C" - "B" - "A" & H.Q. Coys. First Party to pass
   starting point Road Junction. N.20.a.3.2. at 2330 hours. 0730.

5. The following distances will be maintained.
   From Starting Point to Cross Roads - O.15.a.80.70.
   100 yards between Coys. afterwards 100 yards between
   Platoons.

   From Railway Crossing O.10.d.55.60. Coys. will move
   independently to positions, reporting when these are
   taken up to Battn. H.Q. by Runner.

                                            H Cheshire
                                          Lieut & A/Adjt.,
                                        8th (Irish) Battn. K.L.Regt.

Issued at 2300 Hours.

    Copies to :-

            1. 171st Infy. Bde.
            2. C.O.
            3. 2nd-in-Co.
            4. Adjt.
            5. Asst. Adjt.
         6/10. 5 Coys.
           11. Trans. Officer.
           12. Quartermaster.
           13. Medical Officer.
           14. Intell. Officer.
           15. R.S.M.
        16/17. War Diary.
           18. File.

                    -o-o-o-o-o-o-o-

SECRET.   8th (IRISH) BATTN. "THE KING'S" (LIVERPOOL REGT.)   COPY No...62
         ADMINISTRATIVE INSTRUCTIONS ISSUED IN
         ACCORDANCE WITH OPERATION ORDER No.62.
-o-o-o-o-o-o-o-o-o-o-o-o-o-o-o-o-o-o-o-o-o-o-o-o-

16.10.18.

1. DRESS:-   Full Marching Order - Leather Jerkins and
              Steel Helmets will be worn.

2. BLANKETS will be rolled in bundles of 10, labelled and
   delivered to Q.M. Stores by 0630 Hours.

3. Officers Kits will be delivered to Q.M. Stores by 0630 Hours.
   All Trench Shelters and Tents will be dumped by Guard Room
   by 0630 Hours.

4. Lewis Gun Limbers, Cookers, Mess Cart, Maltese Cart, Tool Limber,
   and supply of S.A.A. and Bombs will accompany the Battalion.

5. Unexpended portion of thr days rations will be carried on
   Cookers.

6. Rear Battn. H.Q. and Transport Lines. will remain at present
   location.

                                    Lieut & A/Adjt.,
                                8th (Irish) Battn. K.L.Regt.

Issued at 2300 Hours.
   Copies to all recipients of O.O.62.

-o-o-o-o-o-o-o-

Report on Operations carried out from
17th to 23rd October 1918.

Ref. Sheet. 36 & 37. 1/40.000.

October 17th. The 57th Division passed through the 47th Division. The 171st Infantry Brigade passed through the Left Battalion of the 142nd Infantry Brigade and continued the advance at 0930 Hours in a N.E. direction towards LILLE. This Battalion being in Support with One Coy. at Ref. Sheet.36. O.11.b. One Coy. at FIN DE LA GUERRE. O.17.b. and two Coys. at ESCOBECQUES - O.11.c. Battn. H.Q. at O.17.c.3.7. The advance went well and this Battalion arrived at LE MARAIS - P.4.b. Here the Battalion billeted for the night, the remaining 3 Battalions of the Brigade being in CANTELEU.

Keeping in touch with the forward Battns

October 18th. At 0630 Hours orders were received for this Battalion to pass through and act as Advance Guard to the Division - crossing the Canal, moving through the Southern outskirts of LILLE meeting the advance guards of the 59th Division at FLERS. Ref. Sheet 36. R.2.a. The complete evacuation of LILLE by the enemy having been carried out over-night, no opposition was met with, and the 11th Battn. ROYAL SCOTS FUSILIERS were met in FLERS at 1200 Hours - From this point orders were to keep in Support to the Right Flank of the 59th Division and to keep in touch with the 74th Division who were operating on their Right, and to fill any gap which may occur between the two Divisions. At nightfall the forward troops of the 59th Division had reached the line M.8.d.- M.14.b. and TRESSIN. Our advanced Company was in touch wh with them in ASCQ and the remaining Coys. behind between ASCQ and ANNAPPES.
In accordance with orders the Battalion remained in this Area for the night - "C" Coy. in ASCQ and three Coys. with Battn. H.Q. in ANNAPPES.

October 19th. The advance was resumed at 0800 Hours. This Battn. continuing to follow up the Right Flank of the 59th Division. At 1400 Hours it was found that the 74th Division on the right had stopped on a line from Railway Crossing at Sheet 37. M.15.b.90.35. - to Road 400 Yards East of CHERENG M.22.a.0.1. The 59th Div. Southern Boundary had been altered - creating a gap which was filled by this Battalion. The advance was continued in conjunction with the 59th Division and at nightfall an outpost line was taken up as under:-

"D" Coy. on left in front of CORNET - N.8.b. & d. in touch with 59th Division.
"C" Coy. on Right in front of MOULINEL.
"A" Coy. in Support in Vicinity of TREQUIERE.
"B" Coy. in Reserve - Vicinity M.17.Central.
Battn. H.Q. - M.17.c.4.2.

The 74th Division had also moved forward and touch was established with them over-night N. of HERTAIN.

October 20th. The advance was continued at 0800 Hours with the object of making the line of the SCAULT CANAL and to seize the Bridgeheads. The Southern Boundary of the Brigade ran along the grid M.16.Central - O.16.Central.
The Battalion moved forward to BLANDAIN where Battn. H.Q. were established at N.15.b.60.80. from where Companies moved forward in the following order D. B. A. & C. On learning that the Northern Boundary of the Brigade ran along the grid N.2.Central - O.1.Central. & O.6.Central. "D" Coy. moved to left front and "B" Coy moved up to right front. "A" Coy. supporting "D" and "C" Coy supporting "B" Coy.

- 2 -

Small Patrols of the enemy, both mounted and on foot were encountered in HONNEVAIN - MONT GARNI and Wood in N.6.d. These places were cleared and our forward Companies by Midday had reached the line O.1.Central - O.7.Central - and O.13.Central. where they came under M.G. fire from wood in O.1.d. and O.8.a. and positions West of FROYENNES. Patrols were sent out to gain touch with troops on flanks and it was found that by 1400 Hours the 74th Division on Right had reached a line East of MARQUAIN with their left Post at N.18.d.5.4. but that the 59th Division on left had not advanced until 2 Hours after this Brigade, and it was not until 1700 Hours that they had been able to clear their front of the enemy and establish touch with our left Post at O.1.Central Here the advance was held up for the night. Our Patrols were active and at daybreak it was known that the enemy was still holding the positions in front;

<u>21st October.</u> On the morning of the 21st the 2/6th (Rifle) Battn. K.L.Regt. took over our positions and continued the advance. This Battalion withdrew to Support as follows:-

  "D" & "B" Coys. to MONT GARNI.
  "A" & "C" "   to HONNEVAIN.

The 2/7th K.L.R. afterwards relieved the 2/6th (Rifle) Bn. K.L.R.. On the morning of the 24th October, the front line ran along the main road running through O.2.b. & d. - O.9.a. & c. and O.15.b. and O.16.c. This Battalion remained in above positions. Battn. H.Q. moving up to HONNEVAIN on the morning of the 23rd October. 1918.

Casualties for the whole operations were as follows:-

  Killed.   2/Lieut. F.T. Edwards., M.C.

  Wounded. 9 Other Ranks.

-o-o-o-o-o-o-o-o-o-o-o-o-

Major,
Commanding, 8th (Irish) Battn. K.L.Regt.

1.11.18.

SPECIAL ORDER
by
MAJOR J. W. JONES, MC.,
COMMANDING 8th(IRISH)BATTALION "THE KING'S"(LIVERPOOL REGT).

21.10.18.

The Commanding Officer wishes to congratulate all ranks upon the excellent progress made by the Battalion in yesterday's advance. He is fully alive to the fact that this is due to the determination and energy of all commanders and to the well disciplined and capable response of all other ranks. We have now driven the enemy out of France in this sector, and are upon the soil of Belgium. His ejection from this country will be a speedy one and can only be delayed by the physical limitations of our gallant armies. Victory, complete and overwhelming, is now in sight, and the Commanding Officer is confident that the share of this Battalion in these final operations will be a glorious one, and that all ranks will vie, one with another, in the attempt to add to the undying achievements of the "Liverpool Irish".

Lieut. & A/Adjt.
8th(Irish) Batt. K.L.R.

The foregoing Special Order will be conveyed to all ranks, but on no account must its terms be communicated, wholly or in part, to persons in the United Kingdom, either for circulation privately or in the press.

Lieut. & A/Adjt.
8th(Irish) Batt. K.L.R.

21.10.18.

Secret.   8th (Irish) Battalion   ⑥
          "The King's (Liverpool) Regiment

Ref. Sheet. 37.   October. 24th 1918.

① The 171st Inf. Bde. will be relieved
to-day by the 172nd Inf. Bde in the
right sector of the Divisional front.
② This Batt. will be relieved in
Support by the 2/4th Batt. South Lancs
Regiment
③ 1 Guide per Company & 1 Guide for
Batt. H.Q. will meet incoming Unit
at Level Crossing N.12.c.4.6. at the
following times and guide their
opposite Companies to Billets:-
        A. Coy 1400 hours
        B. . 1430 .
        C. . 1500 .
        D. . 1530 .
        B.H.Q. 1545 .
④ On relief Companies will move
independently to billets at LE FRESNOY

M.10.b. The following distances will be maintained on the march.
  100 yds between platoons.
  300 yds   "   Companies.
(5) Relief complete will be reported to present B.H.Q. by runner.
(6) Lewis Gun Limbers will accompany Companies — All cookers will move to new area at 2.0 p.m.
(7) Billets will be left in a clean condition — Certificates obtained and sent to B.H.Q by 2000 hours.
(8) Provisional Defence Scheme will not be handed over.

                                H. Christie
                                Lieut & Adjt
                                8th K.L.R.

Issued at 12 hours
171. Inf. Bde.
C.O.
Adjt
5. Companies
2/4th S.L.R.
War Diary (2 Copies).
File

SECRET.   Copy No...

War Diary 8th (IRISH) BATTALION "THE KING'S" (LIVERPOOL REGT.)

OPERATION ORDER No.63
-o-o-o-o-o-o-o-o-o-o-o-o-

Ref. Sheets 36 & 37.   29.10.18.
1/40.000.
              (7)

1. The 171st Infantry Brigade will be relieved by the 161st Infantry Brigade to-morrow, 30th October.1918. and will move to the BELLEMEL Area.

2. The Battalion will be relieved by the 18th Battalion LONDON IRISH RIFLES.

3. The Battalion will move by March Route to Billets at (Ref. Sheet.36) M.12.A. - in the order H.Q., A. B. C. D. Coys. - Transport. Leading Coy. will pass Starting Point - Road Junction. (Ref. Sheet.37) M.11.c.75.75. at 0915 hours. 100 Yards distance between Coys. and 100 Yards between "D" Coy. and Transport.

4. Dress:- Full Marching Order - Soft Caps - Steel Helmets strapped on back of Packs.

5. Route via LID - CHERENG - MELLEMEL - Brigade Starting Point is at Sheet 37. M.12.a.4.0.

6. All Defence Instructions - Instructions for the Advance - Aeroplane Photographs and Maps Scale 1/20.000 will be handed over by Rear Party, receipts being obtained and forwarded to Batt. Orderly Room at 2000 hours to-morrow.

7. A C K N O W L E D G E.

                                              Lieut & A/Adjt.
                                           8th (Irish) Battn. K.L.Regt.

Issued at 2115 hours.

Copies to :-

1. 171st Infantry Brigade.
2. Commanding Officer.
3. 2nd-in-Command.
4. Adjutant.
5/9. 5 Coys.
10. T.O.
11. M.O.
12. S.O.
13. Q.M.
14/15. War Diary.
16. R.S.M.
17. File.

-o-o-o-o-o-o-o-o-

8TH (IRISH) BN.
THE KING'S
(LIVERPOOL REGT.)
No. 5243.
Date

SECRET   Copy No...

8th (IRISH) BATTN. "THE KING'S" (LIVERPOOL REGT.)

ADMINISTRATIVE INSTRUCTIONS ISSUED IN
ACCORDANCE WITH OPERATION ORDER No.63.
-o-o-o-o-o-o-o-o-   -o-o-o-o-o-o-o-

                                                          29.10.18.

1. Officers Kits. Mess Kits. Orderly Room Stores. Mens'
   Blankets, rolled tightly in bundles of 10 and labelled
   will be stacked at Q.M. Stores by 0800 hours.

2. Cookers and Lewis Gun Limbers will be ready for Transport
   Officer for 0830 hours.

3. Unexpended portion of the days Rations will be carried on
   Cookers - Dinners will be served on arrival at new Area.

4. Billets will be left in a clean and sanitary condition.
   Certificate being obtained by Rear Party and forwarded to
   this Office by 0900 hours.

5. One Lorry is allotted to this Battalion. Quartermaster will
   send guide for same to present Brigade Headquarters by 0800
   hours to-morrow.

6. Billeting Party consisting of 2/Lieut. T.C. McCarthy -
   1 N.C.O. for Bn.H.Q. - 1 N.C.O. from "A" Coy. - 1 N.C.O. from
   "B" Coy. and 1 N.C.O. from "C" Coy. (who will billet for
   "C" & "D" Coys.) will report to Battn. Orderly Room at
   0815 hours.

7. Rear Party consisting of 2/Lieut. H. Irwin, M.C., R.M. - 1.C.O.
   from Bn.H.Q. - 2 O.Rs. per Company will be left behind to hand
   over and show incoming Unit the Billets. This party will
   report to Battn. Orderly Room at 1000 hours.

8. Rations. Quartermaster will arrange for guide for
   supply wagons at Road Junction Sheet 36. C.12.a.60.65.
   Junction of RUE PIERRE LEGRAND and RUE de CAMBRAY.

                                    H. Cheshire
                                    Lieut & A/Adjt.
                                    8th (Irish) Battn. K.L.Regt.

   Issued at 2115 hours.

        Copies to all recipients of O.O.63.

           -o-o-o-o-o-o-o-o-o-o-o-

8th (Irish) Batt "The King's"
(Liverpool) Regiment.

WAR DIARY
or
INTELLIGENCE SUMMARY.

Army Form C. 2118.

SECRET

NOVEMBER 1918

Place	Date	Hour	Summary of Events and Information	Remarks and references to Appendices
HELLEMES	Nov 1st 1918		Strength Effective 37 Offs. 703 O.R.s Ration 25 " 586 "	
	Nov 11th 1918		Lt Col E.C. HEATH. D.S.O. resumed command of the Batt. vice Major J.F. JONES M.C. GERMANY having intimated her desire for an Armistice was granted it subject to definite conditions laid down by the Allies Armistice signed.	
	Nov 12th 1918		Inspection of Brigade by Major General R.W.R BARNES C.B Commanding 57th DIVISION.	
	Nov 13th–30th 1918		Batn. Coy and Specialist Training.	
	Nov 30th 1918		Strength Effective 36 Offs. 724 O.R.s Ration 29 " 662 "	

Comm 8th (Irish) Batt "The King's" (Liverpool) Regt.
Captain

8th (Irish) Batt.
The King's (Liverpool) Regt.

Army Form C. 2118.

SECRET

WAR DIARY
or
INTELLIGENCE SUMMARY.
(Erase heading not required)

December 1918.

Place	Date 1918	Hour	Summary of Events and Information	Remarks and references to Appendices
HELLEMES LILLE.	1st Dec. 2nd Dec.		Strength. Effective. 26 Off. 704 O.Rs. Ration. 29 Off. 682 O.Rs. Battalion moved by march route to huts East of CARVIN. (Ref. Reno 11. I. L. 80.90.	
CARVIN.	3rd Dec.		Battalion moved by march route to Billets in ARRAS (Ref. Reno 11. 3. I. 18.53.	
ARRAS.	4th Dec.		Captain A.A. Exsbury M.C. assumed command of the Battalion vice Lieut. Col. Eb. Heath D.S.O. who assumed the duties of Brigade Commander.	①
ARRAS.	5th to 24th Dec. 25-26th Dec. 27th Dec.		Training - and Education Classes. Christmas Holiday. Battalion moved by march route to huts at BERNEVILLE (Ref. Reno 11. 3. I. 05.22.	
BERNEVILLE	29th Dec. 28-31st Dec. 31st Dec.		Lieut. Col. Eb. Heath D.S.O. resumed command of the Battalion. Training - Education Classes - Salvage Work. Strength. Effective 39 Off. 719 O.R. Ration 30 Off. 605 O.R. 21 Men sent to England for demobilization during the month.	

Comm'd of 8th (Irish) Batt. The King's (L'pool) Regt.

[signature]
Lieut. Colonel

SECRET

8th (IRISH) BATTALION. "THE KING 'S" (LIVERPOOL REGT.)

OPERATION ORDER No.64.

Ref. Maps:-
TOURNAI. 3.
LENS.11.

30.11.18.

1. The Battalion will move to ARRAS Area on Monday, December 2nd and Tuesday, 3rd December, 1918.

2. The Battalion will stage for the night of December 2nd in the CARVIN AREA.

3. The Battalion will parade in "BATTLE ORDER" (Soft Caps will be worn) on road leading to Factory at 0805 Hours. Company Markers will report to R.S.M. at 0705 Hours at Bat tn. Orderly Room.
Order of March will be :- Band, H.Q.,A.B.C.D. Coys. and Transport.

4. ROUTE :- LEZENNES - NONGHIN - LESQUIN - TEMPLEMARS - MOULIN.
Starting Point :- R.13.c.2b.9. (Cross-Roads LEZENNES)
This will be passed at 0840 Hours.

5. The following intervals will be maintained :-

    Between Battns :- 500 Yds.
         " Coys. :- 100 "
         " Battn & Transport:- 100 Yds.

6. Battn. H.Q. will close on December 2nd & 3rd at 0800 Hrs and re-open at CARVIN & ARRAS immediately on arrival. Messages on the march will be sent to the head of the column.

7. O.C. Coys. will report in person immediately their men are settled in Billets.

8. ACKNOWLEDGE.

                                    2/Lieut & Actg. Adjt.,
                                    8th (Irish) Battn. K.L.Regt.

Issued at 1800 Hrs.
30.11.18.

Copies to :-

    1. 171st Infy. Bde.
    2. C.O.
    3. 2nd-in-Cd.
    4. Adjt.
    5/8. 4 Coys.
    10. T.O.
    11. Q.M.
    12. R.S.M.
    13. Sig. Officer.
    14/15. War Diary.
    16. File.

SECRET.   COPY NO...
            8th (IRISH) BATTALION. "THE KING'S" (LIVERPOOL REGT.)

                    ADMINISTRATIVE INSTRUCTIONS ISSUED IN
                    ACCORDANCE WITH OPERATION ORDER No.64.
            ----

1. **BILLETING.** Capt. J.F. Worrall., M.C. and 1 N.C.O. per Coy. will report to this office at 0730 Hrs on December 2nd.

2. Officers Valises, Mess Kit, Men's Packs and Blankets will be dumped outside Q.M.Stores by 0700 Hrs. Blankets will be rolled in bundles of ten and labelled clearly.

3. Billets will be left in a clean and sanitary condition. The 2nd-in-Command will inspect billets at 0730 Hours and obtain clean certificate from the Town Major.

4. Cookers & Lewis Gun Limbers will be ready for the Transport Officer by 0730 Hours.

5. The unexpended portion of the days rations will be carried on the Cookers.

6. Valises and Blankets will be drawn from the Quartermaster on arrival at CARVIN.

                                            J McConnely
                                            2/Lt. & Actg., Adjt.
                                            8th (Irish) Battn. K.L.Regt.

Issued at 1800 Hours.
    To all recipients of O.O.64.

SECRET.   8th (IRISH) BATTALION. "THE KING'S" (LIVERPOOL REGIMENT).   COPY No.

OPERATION ORDER No. 65
-o-o-o-o-o-o-o-o-o-o-o-o-o-o-o-o-o-

26.12.18.

1. The Battalion will move to Camp at GRANDVILLE to-morrow, 27th December. 1918.

2. The Battalion will parade in Full Marching Order (Soft Caps will be worn) in Barrack Square at 0945 Hours.
Coy. Markers will report to R.S.M. at 0935 Hours - Coys. will be steady on Markers at 0940 Hrs.
Order of March will be :- H.Q. - A. B. C. D Coys. Transport.

3. Starting Point - G.26.b.78. This will be passed at 1000 Hrs.

4. The following intervals will be maintained :-

    Between Coys.   100 Yds.
    "   Battn. & Transport- 100 Yds.

5. Battn. H.Q. will close on December 27th at 0945 Hrs and re-open immediately on arrival at New Camp. Messages on the march will be sent to head of the column.

6. O.C. Coys. will report in person immediately their men are settled in Billets.

                                    J. McCarthy
                                    2/Lieut & Actg., Adjt.,
                                    8th (Irish) Battn. K.L.R.

Issued at 1800 Hrs.
    Copies to :-

        1.   171st Infy. Bde.
        2.   C.O.
        3.   Adjt.,
        4.   Sig. Off.
        5.   T.O.
        6.   Q.M.
        7/11. 5 Coys.
        12. R.S.M.
        13/14. War Diary.
        15. File.

-o-o-o-o-o-

8th (Irish) Battalion.
The Kings (Liverpool) Regiment

January 1919
"8 Liverpool R"
"SECRET."
Army Form C. 2118.

WAR DIARY
or
INTELLIGENCE SUMMARY.
(Erase heading not required.)

Instructions regarding War Diaries and Intelligence Summaries are contained in F. S. Regs., Part II. and the Staff Manual respectively. Title pages will be prepared in manuscript.

Place	Date	Hour	Summary of Events and Information	Remarks and references to Appendices
BERNEVILLE Rue Kuo N. 13.I.05.22.	1919 Jany. 1st.		Strength – Effective 39. Offs. 719. O.Rs, Ration 30. Offs 605. O.Rs Training – Education Classes – Competitions and Games carried out daily during the month. 5 Officers and 140 O.Rs sent to England for Demobilization during the month.	
	Jany. 25th.		Lieut. Col. E.b. Heath, D.S.O. having proceeded to England on leave the command of the Battalion was assumed by Capt. J.E. Smitham M.C.	
	Jany. 31st.		Strength Effective 33. Officers 560. O.Rs. Ration 23 440	

[signature]
Captain
Commdg. 8th (Irish) Battn.
The Kings (Liverpool) Regt.

8 SECRET
8 Liverpool
February 1919.

Army Form C. 2118.

WAR DIARY
or
INTELLIGENCE SUMMARY
(Erase heading not required)

8TH (IRISH) BN. "THE KING'S" (LIVERPOOL REGT.)

Instructions regarding War Diaries and Intelligence Summaries are contained in F.S. Regs., Part II. and the Staff Manual respectively. Title pages will be prepared in manuscript.

Place	Date	Hour	Summary of Events and Information	Remarks and references to Appendices
BERNEVILLE Troop Ref. Q.6.d.8.9 Sheet 51.C.	1st to 28th FEB. 1919.		1st Feb:- Effective Strength. 36 Offrs 695. Other Ranks. Ration Strength. 23 Offrs. 444 Other Ranks. Training – Education – Classes & Salvage Work. 28th Feb: Effective Strength. 19 Offrs. 193 Other Ranks. Ration Strength. 9 Offrs 61 Other Ranks. 4 Offrs + 250 men Demobilised during month. 4 Offrs + 200 men Transferred to 25th Bn. K.L.R.	

C. E. Booth
LIEUT-COLONEL
COMMANDING 8th (IRISH) BATTN. "THE KING'S" (LIVERPOOL) REGT.

[Stamp: B/H (IRISH) BN. "THE KING'S" (LIVERPOOL REGT.) No. 9318 Date 15/3/19]

Army Form C. 2118.

WAR DIARY
or
INTELLIGENCE SUMMARY.

(Erase heading not required.)

SECRET

MARCH 1919.

WO 26

Place	Date	Hour	Summary of Events and Information	Remarks and references to Appendices
BERNEVILLE Map Ref 4.6 d. 8.9 Sheet 51.c.	1/3/19 to 17/3/19		1st March. {Effective Strength 19 Offrs 193. O.Rs. {Ration Strength 9 Offrs 61. O.Rs. Training & Salvage Work.	
	18/3/19		Battalion "Cadre" moved by March Route to MARQUION	
MARQUION Map Ref F.2.c.4.6. Sheet 51.c.	19/3/19 to 31/3/19		Training 31st March. {Effective Strength 6 Offrs 52 O.Rs. {Ration Strength 6 Offrs 49 O.Rs. 4 Offrs 22. O.Rs demobilised during month 4 Offrs H.O.Rs transferred to 59th Division.	

J. M. M^c...
LIEUT.-COLONEL
COMMANDING 8th (IRISH) BATTN. "THE KING'S" (LIVERPOOL) REGT.

SECRET.

8th (IRISH) BATTALION. "THE KING'S" (LIVERPOOL REGIMENT).

OPERATION ORDER No. 160.

Map. Ref. 51.C.   17.3.19.

1. This Battalion will move to the Huts allotted in the Camp of the 9th K.L.R. at MAROEUIL, to-morrow, 18th inst.

2. The Battalion will parade on the Parade Ground at 1000 Hours. Dress:- Full Marching Order.

3. Officers Valises, Mess Kit etc will be dumped outside the Officers Mess by 0900 Hours. Blankets will be rolled in bundles of 10 and clearly labelled.

4. Animals will be stabled in the Horse Lines of the 9th K.L.R. at ETRUN. Vehicles will be parked in vicinity of Camp.

5. Lamps and Wash Basins will be handed over to Q.M. by 0900 Hours.

6. Capt. F.W. Hogg will detail a loading party of 1 N.C.O. & 5 men to report to the Q.M. by 0900 Hrs to-morrow. This party will remain behind to clear up the Camp. Lieut. W.W. Redding will be i/c of this Party.

7. Huts will be left in a clean and sanitary condition.

8. Battn. H.Q. will close at EKMAVILLE at 1000 Hrs and re-open immediately on arrival at new camp.

Capt & Adjt.,
8th (Irish) Battn. K.L.Regt.

Issued at 1500 Hrs.
17.3.19.

Headquarters.
57th Division.

SECRET.
~~SECRET~~

Herewith War Diary for the Month of April, 1919, please.

[Stamp: 8TH (IRISH) BN. / "THE KING'S" / (LIVERPOOL REGT.) / No. 2657 / Date 5.5.19.]

                    J. W. Conway Capt.
                                    Major,
Commdg. 8th (Irish) Bn. K.L.R.

SECRET Army Form C. 2118.

WAR DIARY
or
INTELLIGENCE SUMMARY
(Erase heading not required.)

8 Liverpool Regt

April 1919

Place	Date	Hour	Summary of Events and Information	Remarks and references to Appendices
MAREUIL	1st		1st April. Effective Strength. 6 Offrs 52 O.Rs.	
Insp. Pol	to		Ration Strength. 6 Offrs 49 O.Rs	
L.2.c.4.6	30th		Training + Fatigues.	
Sheet 51.C.				
			30th April. Effective Strength. 6 Offrs 48 O.Rs.	
			Ration Strength. 6 Offrs 48 O.Rs.	
			4. O.Rs to England for Demobilisation	
			M/R. L.C. ASHTON, MC. attd from 57th Div. Reception Camp to Eng. for Demob.	

Total 27

J. .... Cut
Major
COMMANDING 8th (IRISH) BATTN. "THE KING'S" (LIVERPOOL) REGT.

Headquarters,
57th Division.

-o-o-o-o-o-o-o-

SECRET.

Herewith War Diary for the Month of
~~JUNE~~ MAY, 1919., please.

for McCunny Capt

Commdg, 8th (Irish) Bn. K.L.R.
Major,

1.6.19.

SECRET   Army Form C. 2118.

Original
WAR DIARY
or
INTELLIGENCE SUMMARY.

8 Liverpool R[egt]

MAY 1919

Instructions regarding War Diaries and Intelligence
Summaries are contained in F. S. Regs., Part II.
and the Staff Manual respectively. Title pages
will be prepared in manuscript.

(Erase heading not required.)

Place	Date	Hour	Summary of Events and Information	Remarks and references to Appendices
MARŒUIL	1st May		Effective Strength 6 offrs 48 O.Rs	
Mnp. Raf	16		Ration Strength 6 offrs 48 ORs	
h.Z.C.4.6	d		Training & Fatigues	
Shut.S.C.	31 d			
	31 May		Effective Strength 3 offrs 18 O Rs	
			Ration Strength 3 offrs 24 O Rs	
			S. O. Rs to bng. for Demob. during month	
			Lt (A/Capt) A. W. Hotchkiss ⎫	
			Lt. W. W. Redding ⎬ To bng. for Demob.	
			Lt. A.E.A. Brown ⎭	

[Signature]
Major
COMMANDING 8 LIVERPOOL REGT

www.ingramcontent.com/pod-product-compliance
Lightning Source LLC
Chambersburg PA
CBHW081404160426
43193CB00013B/2100